ACT
As God's Children

The Word Is Life

Rev. Gerard P. Weber
Rev. James J. Killgallon
Sr. M. Michael O'Shaughnessy, O.P.

Benziger
A division of Benziger Bruce & Glencoe, Inc.
Encino, California

Nihil Obstat:
  Robert R. Monahan, O.F.M.
  Censor Deputatus

Imprimatur:
  †William Cardinal Baum
  Archbishop of Washington
  December 6, 1976

Nihil Obstat:
  Austin B. Vaughan, S.T.D.

Imprimatur:
  †James P. Mahoney, D.D.
  Vicar General
  Archdiocese of New York
  September 13, 1972

The nihil obstat and imprimatur are official declarations that a book or pamphlet is free of doctrinal or moral error. No implication is contained therein that those who have granted the nihil obstat and imprimatur agree with the contents, opinions or statements expressed.

Copyright © 1977, 1973 by Benziger Bruce & Glencoe, Inc. All rights reserved. No part of this book may be reproduced or transmitted in any form or by any means, electronic or mechanical, including photocopying, recording, or by any information storage and retrieval system, without permission in writing from the Publisher.

Benziger
A division of Benziger Bruce & Glencoe, Inc.
17337 Ventura Boulevard
Encino, California 91316
Collier Macmillan Canada, Ltd.

Printed in the United States of America.

Contents

We Care for the World, the World Cares for Us   6

  1. Our Work This Year 8
  2. The Gift of Life 14
  3. God Gives the Animals to Man 22
  4. Peter Finds a Friend 28
  5. God Puts the World in Man's Hands ... 36
  6. Emily's First Apple 42
  7. "Because the Moon Is There!" 48
      Review 54

God's Laws and Ourselves   56

  8. Billy Goes to Visit Strange Worlds 58
  9. Anything Goes! 66
10. The State of Violence 72
11. Crooksville 78
12. The Land of Try Anything Once 84
13. Billy Comes Back to Earth 92
14. "Love God with Your Whole Heart" ... 96
15. "Love Your Neighbor as Yourself" ... 102
16. "I Think You're Beginning to Grow Up" ... 108
      Review 114

We Are Loved By God   116

17. Let Your Conscience Be Your Guide 118
18. "Honor Your Father and Your Mother".......124
19. Together We Are Strong 128
20. The Tongue Is A Gift from God 134
21. "You Shall Not Bear False Witness" 140
22. Share with One Anther 144
23. "Lord, Teach Us How to Pray" 148
24. Let Us Pray 152
25. "I Am Sorry" 156
    Review 160

Special People, Special Times   162

A Birthday for Mary 164
People of Light: Christmas 166
Groundhogs, Candles and Wolves 170
Fishbones and Blessings 172
Patrick in the Halls of Tara: Easter 176
Game 180
Prayers 182

ACT

1 We Care for the World, the World Cares for Us

1. Our Work This Year

Signs Tell Us Something

"Go!"
"Please Walk on the Grass!"
"Come on In!"
"Swim Here!"

It would be nice if we saw signs like these everywhere. But these are not signs that we often see. We usually see signs that say:

"Stop!"
"Please Keep off the Grass!"
"Keep Out!"
"No Swimming!"

Why do signs so often tell us what *not* to do? If we look at the signs again and study them, we may find the answer.

The sign that says "Stop!" may keep us from running into the street. In the street, we might be hit by a car.

The sign that says "Keep off the Grass!" tells us that the lawn is new. We might kill the young grass if we walk on it now. The sign asks us to give the grass a chance to grow. Then everyone can walk and play on it someday.

The sign that says "Keep Out!" tells us of danger. It might mean that there are live wires or machines here. These things could hurt or kill us.

The "No Swimming!" sign is not there to spoil our fun. It is there to warn us. It tells us that this part of the beach or shore is dangerous. Anyone who disobeys this sign might lose his life.

Growing Up Means Learning

A little two-year-old baby seems to be everywhere. He seems to have more than two hands. He reaches for cups, glasses, papers, magazines. He will grab anything within his reach. The rest of the family is busy moving things out of the baby's reach. They are always saying "No, no" or "You can't have that." The baby does not understand.

Older people understand. The baby is too young to know how to treat things. He would break the cup or the glass. He would upset the papers. He would chew on the magazines. These things are there to be used by people who know how to use them properly.

A little child does not understand why his parents will not let him have a puppy or a kitten. A child sees a tiny animal as something to play with. But the parents know that an animal is a living thing. An animal can feel pain. It needs to be fed and taken care of. A little child is too young to understand how to take care of a pet. When he is older, the child can have a pet. Then he will know how to care for it.

Babies and very young children only hear "No, no." They do not understand. As we grow up, we come to understand that growing up means learning how to use things. It means finding out why we may or may not do certain things. It means learning the reasons why some actions are "right" and some are "wrong."

God our Father gave us wonderful bodies. He gave us wonderful minds. He also gave us a beautiful world to grow up in. This year, we will look at ourselves. We will look at the world God has given us. We will think about what we do and what we do not do, as boys and girls who are growing up where we are. We will think about how we act and why we act. These things are important to us because we belong to our family and to God's big family—the family of man.

Stop and Think

This year, we are going to learn how and why we do things as Christians:

1. Did you do something today that made someone happy?

2. How did you do it?

3. Why did you do it?

For Home and School

1. Ask your parents about how you have grown and changed since you have been in school.

2. Ask your parents **why** you are still growing and changing.

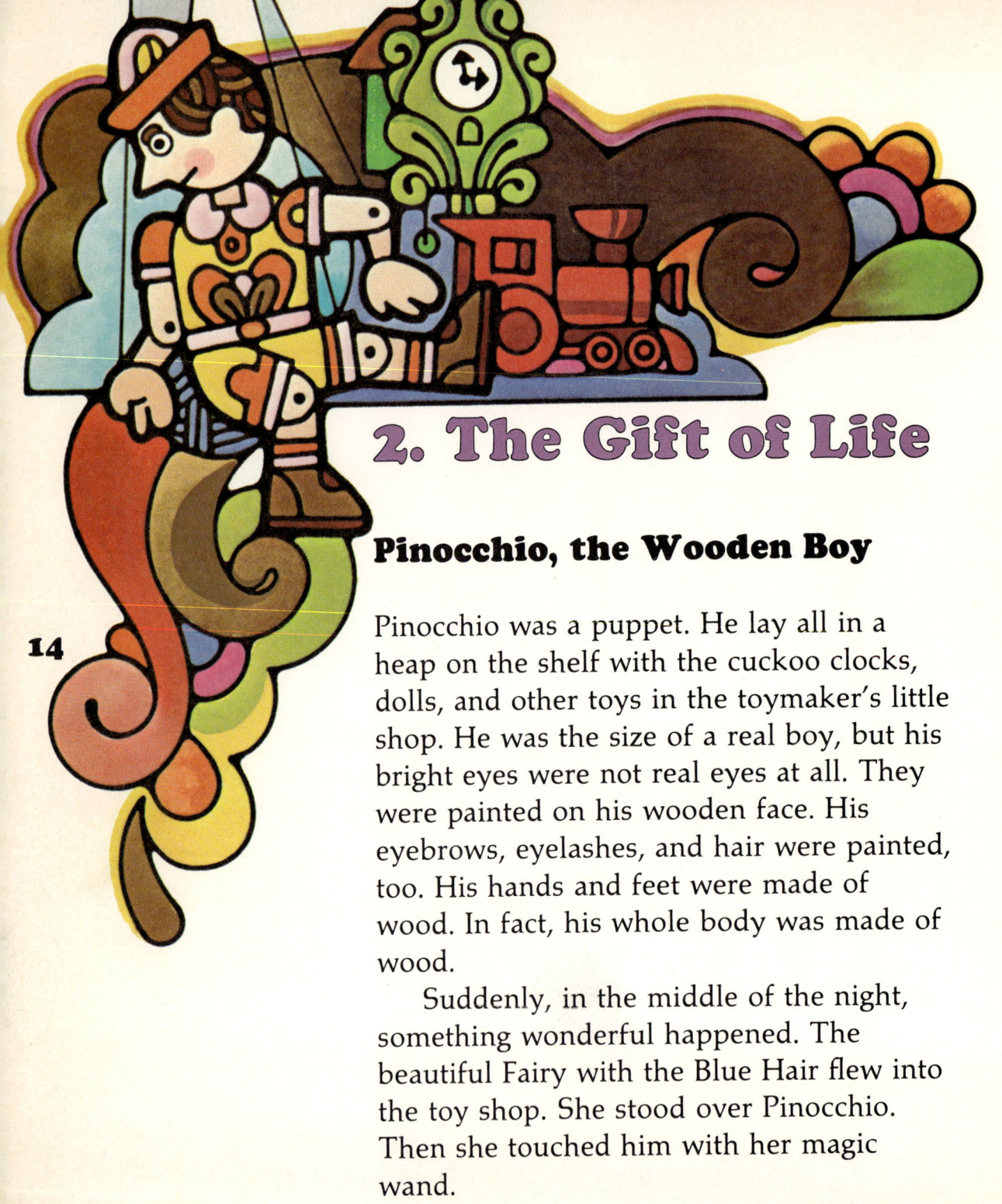

2. The Gift of Life

Pinocchio, the Wooden Boy

Pinocchio was a puppet. He lay all in a heap on the shelf with the cuckoo clocks, dolls, and other toys in the toymaker's little shop. He was the size of a real boy, but his bright eyes were not real eyes at all. They were painted on his wooden face. His eyebrows, eyelashes, and hair were painted, too. His hands and feet were made of wood. In fact, his whole body was made of wood.

Suddenly, in the middle of the night, something wonderful happened. The beautiful Fairy with the Blue Hair flew into the toy shop. She stood over Pinocchio. Then she touched him with her magic wand.

Pinocchio sat up. He rubbed his painted eyes with his wooden hands. His eyes could see now. His ears could hear. He could even speak. He was alive!

The fairy spoke to Pinocchio. "The toymaker wished on a star," she said. "He wanted you to be alive, little wooden boy. So I have come to give you the gift of life."

Pinocchio was so excited he could hardly breathe. "I am alive!" he shouted. "I can walk!"

But then a big question came into Pinocchio's wooden head. There was something he had to know. "Am I—am I—a real boy?" he asked the fairy.

"Oh, no," the fairy said. "You are alive, but you are only a wooden boy. You are not a real boy with flesh and blood and a real heart."

"But I wish I could be a real boy," Pinocchio said.

"Maybe you can become a real boy someday," the Fairy with the Blue Hair told him.

"How? How? What do I have to do to become a real boy?" Pinocchio shouted.

The fairy said, "You will have to find out who you really are and who you really want to be. And you will have to do something brave and unselfish. You will have to think about someone besides yourself. You will have to help someone."

Pinocchio Tries to Become a Real Boy

Pinocchio made up his mind that he would try very hard to become a real boy. But it was not easy. Pinocchio was only a puppet. He did not know right from wrong. He did not want to go to school. He did not want to do what the toymaker told him to do. He did not know how to be kind to people.

A little cricket hopped into the toy shop one day. The cricket tried to help Pinocchio. He told him what he should do and what he should not do. But Pinocchio often refused to listen to the cricket.

Every time Pinocchio disobeyed and did wrong, something happened to him. When Pinocchio lied, his nose grew. It became longer each time he lied. And when Pinocchio did foolish things, his ears grew long. They grew into donkey's ears.

Sometimes Pinocchio ran away instead of going to school. When he did this, his friends suffered. Once, the old toymaker went to search for him and was swallowed by a whale. The Fairy with the Blue Hair was sad about the way Pinocchio misbehaved. She became very ill.

Finally, Pinocchio stopped thinking only of himself. He began to think about others. He set out to find the toymaker. He risked his own life to rescue the old man from the belly of the whale. Then Pinocchio went to work. He wove baskets day and night to earn money for the toymaker.

Pinocchio Receives a Reward

Then, after he had worked extra hard one day, Pinocchio fell asleep. He had a wonderful dream. He dreamed that the Fairy with the Blue Hair bent over and kissed him. She said: "My good Pinocchio! Because of your kind heart, I forgive you all your bad deeds. Boys who help other people so willingly and lovingly deserve praise. Always listen to good advice, and you will be happy."

Then the dream ended, and Pinocchio woke up. Imagine his surprise, now, to discover that he was no longer a wooden puppet! Instead, he had become a real boy.

Pinocchio threw his arms around the toymaker's neck. "What has happened, Father?" he cried. "How have these wonderful things come about?"

"It is your reward for your change of conduct," the old toymaker replied. "When people stop being bad and try to be good, they make the whole household happy."

"And the old wooden Pinocchio," the boy asked, "where has he gone?"

"There he is," the old man answered. He pointed to a limp, lifeless wooden doll.

Pinocchio looked at it for a moment. Then he said to himself with great satisfaction, "How funny I was when I was a puppet! And how glad I am to be a real boy at last!

Stop and Think

Pinocchio learned what he had to do to become real. He listened very carefully to kind advice and he was unselfish:

1. Can you remember a time when you wanted something very badly?

2. Did you try to be very good so that you would get what you wanted?

3. Can you remember a time when you felt very good because you were brave or unselfish?

For Home and School

1. The old toymaker said to Pinocchio, "When people stop being bad and try to be good, they make the whole household happy." Talk to your parents about this sentence.

2. List two brave and unselfish people that you know about. Ask your parents to talk with you about why these people are brave and unselfish.

3. God Gives the Animals to Man

Samuel Has a Question

The black sky over the desert seemed to be alive with bright, twinkling stars. Samuel looked up at them in wonder.

This was the time Samuel liked best. He was sitting by the campfire with the other boys and girls. The children were listening to an old man they called "Uncle Jacob." All the children loved him. He was one of the oldest men in the whole camp, and he told the best stories.

Every night the children would gather around the fire with Uncle Jacob. This was the hour they all loved. The days were long. All the people, even the children, walked all day through the dry, hot desert. They carried their clothes and household belongings with them. Finally, in the late afternoon, they would stop.

Tonight, sitting near the fire, Samuel was especially happy. The stars were so beautiful. He seemed to be seeing them for the first time. Suddenly, Samuel wondered about something he had never thought of before. He knew the word for the stars— the Hebrew word, "akokaveem." But now Samuel wondered who first thought of naming the stars and the other things in the world.

Samuel couldn't keep still any longer. "Uncle Jacob," he asked, "who gave the stars, the animals and other things their names?"

Uncle Jacob Tells a Story

"There is a wonderful story about that," Uncle Jacob said. "It is an old, old story. Our people have told it over and over again as long as anyone can remember. It is part of the story that our people tell when they talk about how God made the world."

The children became very quiet. Then Uncle Jacob began to speak. "After God made the world, He made a man—Adam. One of the first things God asked Adam to do was to give names to all creation. And he asked Adam to name the animals first. Why do you think God did that?"

"Was it because God wanted Adam to know that He had made the animals to help man?" one of the boys asked.

"That is right," Uncle Jacob said. "Adam was to take care of the animals. That is why God told Adam to name the animals. By giving the animals their names, Adam showed that he was in charge of them and knew them."

Uncle Jacob went on with his story. "It was fun to think up names for the animals. 'That one with the long neck is really funny,' Adam said to himself. 'It should have a funny name. I will call it a giraffe! That strange animal with the black and white stripes is funny, too. I'll call him a zebra. That one over there can give milk. I will call her a cow.'

" 'That one who comes running to me wagging its tail is especially smart and friendly,' Adam thought. 'He can help me herd the sheep. I will call him a dog.'

"Adam spent a long and busy time naming the animals," Uncle Jacob said, "but he was happy. He remembered the words God had said to him. God meant these words for all men who would later live on the earth:

> Have mastery over the fish of the sea, the birds of the air, and all the living things that move on earth.

"When God told Adam to name the animals," Uncle Jacob said, "God was telling him to take care of the animals. Adam was to feed the horses and the cattle and the dogs and the cats. He was to give them shelter. He was to protect the wild animals. He was not to hurt them. He was not to kill them unless it was necessary."

The children always remembered what Uncle Jacob said at the end of his story. He said, "Adam was a better man, he was more a man, because he cared for the animals God had put on the earth with him and for him."

Stop and Think

This chapter told about being better persons by treating animals well.

1. What are some things you have named?

2. How do you take care of your pets or other animals?

3. Why do you take care of them?

For Home and School

1. Talk to your parents about their experiences with animals.

2. Ask your parents how we care for animals. How do we become better boys and girls by caring for animals?

4. Peter Finds a Friend

"I Don't Care!"

Peter was in trouble.
This time it was school. His teacher kept him after class. She looked very sternly at Peter. In a very firm voice she told him, "You are not to come back to this school until you bring your mother with you! You have fought with every single boy in this class! You are disobedient and bold in class! You are failing in every single subject!"

The teacher looked sadly at Peter. Then, she said the terrible words: "I'm afraid we haven't found any way we can do anything with you or for you, Peter."

When the teacher said these words, Peter put on a hard face and shrugged his shoulders. He pretended he didn't care. He'd show everybody. He didn't need anybody. He'd get along all by himself.

But Peter was not really happy as he said these words to himself. He felt very sad. He was lonely.

Peter lived with his mother in a very small apartment in a run-down part of the city. He had never seen his father. His mother worked all day. She got home only just in time to give Peter his supper. Sometimes she had to work in the evenings, too. Then she would leave Peter a note saying, "Peter, I won't be home until late. Take this change and go out and get a hot dog for your supper."

A Friend in Need

One afternoon after school, Peter came bursting into the gloomy apartment. It was quiet and empty, as usual. His mother was not home. Instead, there was a note with a quarter and a dime, enough money to buy a hot dog for supper.

Peter scooped up the change. He turned around and raced down the steps and into the street. "OK," he thought to himself. "I'm all alone, but I've got something to do. There's a vacant old building on the corner. They'll tear it down soon. I'll go explore it."

Peter ran down to the building and went in. It was cold and dark but Peter started to explore it anyway.

Tearing wallpaper off the walls in one of the old apartments was fun for a while. Then Peter found some loose boards. He amused himself by pulling them out.

Suddenly Peter stood quite still. What was that sound coming from behind that loose board?

There it was again!

"Meow!"

Then Peter stooped down and looked into the space behind the broken wall. There he saw a frightened kitten.

"Hey, little guy, you're hungry, aren't you? I'll bet you're real hungry," Peter said.

"Meeooow," the kitten answered.

Peter was hungry, too. He had thirty-five cents in his pocket, money for his hot dog. But the kitten was hungrier than he was, Peter thought. It was smaller, too. It had even fewer friends than Peter had.

Peter made up his mind. He put the kitten down on the floor, very gently. "You stay here," he said. "I'm going to get you something to eat. I'll be right back."

Peter's thirty-five cents was enough to buy a can of cat food and a pint of milk at the store. He stopped at his place to borrow a can opener and a dish from the kitchen. Then he rushed back to the empty apartment. The kitten had not gone back into the hole in the wall.

Peter opened the can of cat food. He poured some milk in the dish.

"Shucks! I don't mind going without supper. I'd rather have you get something into your skinny little body," Peter said to his new friend.

"Dusty!" Peter cried. "I'm going to call you Dusty because you're gray-looking. And you and I are going to be friends!"

Peter Changes

One afternoon, Peter's mother found two cans of cat food in the refrigerator. "That's funny," she thought. "We don't have a cat. This must be something Peter is up to." And so Peter's secret came out. He had to tell his mother all about Dusty. He said that he had been caring for the kitten and feeding it for three weeks.

"And now I'm worried about Dusty," Peter told his mother. "It's getting colder. There's no heat in that old building. I—I—Mom, do you think? Could we? . . ."

Peter's mother went over and put her arm around Peter. "Peter," she said, "you have to take care of pets, and it's a lot of trouble. But if you promise to take care of Dusty, you can bring your kitten home and keep it." Peter was filled with happiness!

A few weeks later, at a parent-teacher meeting, Peter's teacher was talking to Peter's mother. "I've never seen such a change in a boy," the teacher said. "Peter behaves in class. He is friendly now. He gets along with the other boys and girls. His marks are much better. He's acting more grown up, more like a real person. I can't understand it."

But Peter's mother understood what had brought about the change in her son. Peter had learned to care about something. He forgot about himself because he felt sorry for the kitten. He found out that he *loved* something—the kitten. He found out that the kitten wanted to be with him.

The kitten helped Peter to see what it means to love and to be wanted. It helped him to understand what it means to care for others and to have others be grateful. Because Peter loved Dusty, Peter opened up. He began to see that if he cared about people, they would care about him, too.

Stop and Think

Peter learned a good lesson. When he found Dusty, he became a better person. He found much more than a kitten. He found out how to be unselfish and how to care:

1. How have you shown kindness and unselfishness?

2. Why did you act this way?

3. What have you learned by caring for something?

For Home and School

1. Doing kind things for people and for all of God's creatures helps us to grow. That is what happened to Peter. Write a story about Peter in the days ahead and how he kept on growing and changing. Ask your parents to help you.

2. Knowing that some people really love and understand us helps us to grow. How do our parents, our teachers, and other grown-ups help us grow?

5. God Puts the World in Man's Hands

Mrs. Clark Tells a Story

The children were standing on the steps in front of the house. There was no place to sit down. The steps and the grass were still wet. It had been raining all afternoon.

But now the rain had stopped. The sky was clean and blue. The sun was breaking through. And there in the sky was a wonderful rainbow. The beautiful colors stretched out in a long line across the sky.

The children were filled with delight. "A rainbow is wonderful," Mary said.

"That is true," Mary's mother said. "But to me a rainbow is something more. To me, a rainbow is a reminder of something."

The children all turned to look at Mary's mother. One of the girls asked the question that was in everyone's mind. "What does the rainbow remind you of, Mrs. Clark?"

"It reminds me of the story the Bible tells about Noah and the ark," Mrs. Clark

said. "You all know the story, don't you?" Most of the children nodded. They remembered the story about the great flood.

"But what about the rainbow?" one of the girls asked. "I remember that story about the flood and the ark and the animals," she said. "But I don't remember anything about a rainbow."

Mrs. Clark smiled. "The rainbow is the best part of the story," she said.

"Tell us about the rainbow!" the children cried.

"Yes, Mother, please," Mary begged. "Tell us while we can still see the rainbow here in the sky."

A New Start

"All right," Mrs. Clark said. "You all know why the Bible tells us the story about Noah and the great flood, don't you?"

"Yes," one of the older girls answered. "The story tells us that God wiped out sin and washed the world clean. It tells us that God saved Noah and his family and the animals Noah took into the ark."

"That's right," Mrs. Clark said. "The story really tells us that God gave the world a new beginning."

Then Mary asked, "Why did the world need a new beginning?"

One of the boys spoke up. "I know," he said. "People had spoiled the world because they were mean and selfish. They didn't care about God or each other."

"That's right," Mrs. Clark said. "God gave us a beautiful, clean, bright, shining world. But men and women were selfish and cruel. They sinned and spoiled the wonderful world God gave them."

"And God washed the world clean because He wanted to give it a new start?" one of the boys asked.

"Yes," Mrs. Clark said. "God's People, the Israelites, knew the old stories about a great flood. They saw this flood as God's way of washing the world clean of sin and evil."

The Sign of the Rainbow

The girl who had asked about the rainbow still wanted to know. "But what about the rainbow?" she asked again.

Mrs. Clark said, "The Bible tells us that after the flood was over, God put His beautiful rainbow in the sky. Noah and his family saw the rainbow as a sign from God."

"A sign of what?" one of the little boys asked.

"A sign that God wouldn't destroy anything again," Mrs. Clark said. "The rainbow was a sign that God was leaving the world in our hands."

"Then the rainbow reminds us that we have to take care of God's world," Mary said. "Then God must trust us a lot if He put His world in our hands.

"Yes," Mrs. Clark agreed. "God gave us a beautiful world, and we must not spoil it. We should help make the world even more beautiful."

All the children nodded. They looked at the beautiful rainbow again. For them, too, it would always be a reminder.

Stop and Think

God gave Noah the rainbow to show His care for the world. He said that He would not flood the world anymore:

1. What are some things that remind you that God wants you to care for the world?

2. What can you do to keep the world beautiful?

For Home and School

1. List projects you can do as a class to keep your classroom neat and clean. Then talk with your parents about how you can keep your home and neighborhood neat and clean.

2. Ask your parents to tell you ways in which the leaders of your city, state, and country are helping to keep our land clean and beautiful. Share your findings with your class.

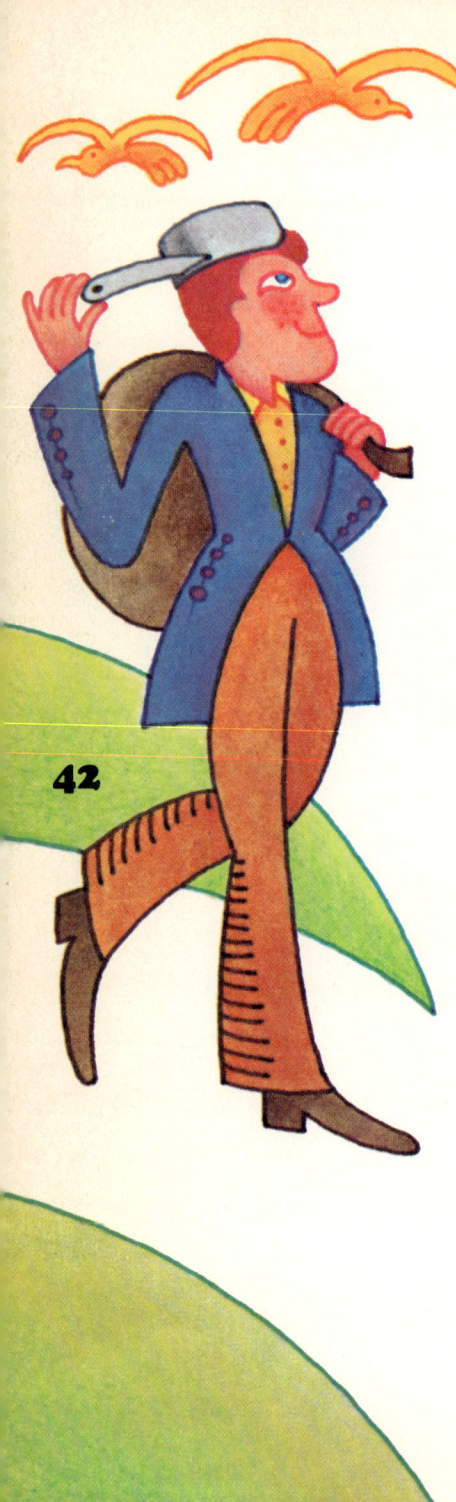

6. Emily's First Apple

Emily's Wish

Emily was lonely. She sat alone under the big oak tree next to the family's log cabin. In Ohio, where Emily was living, there were forests and wide open spaces, wolves and Indians. There were only a few families like Emily's. And no other family lived close by.

Emily's mother and father often told her about what it was like to live in Boston. Emily closed her eyes and remembered what her mother had told her. She was in a park. It was spring. There was a wonderful smell in the air. It was the smell of apple blossoms. Emily closed her eyes tighter. She tried to imagine the beautiful pink flowers that grew on the apple trees.

Emily had never seen an apple tree. She had never even tasted an apple. Her mother and father had told her about the taste of juicy red apples. Her mouth watered as she remembered what they had said about the taste of hot apple pie.

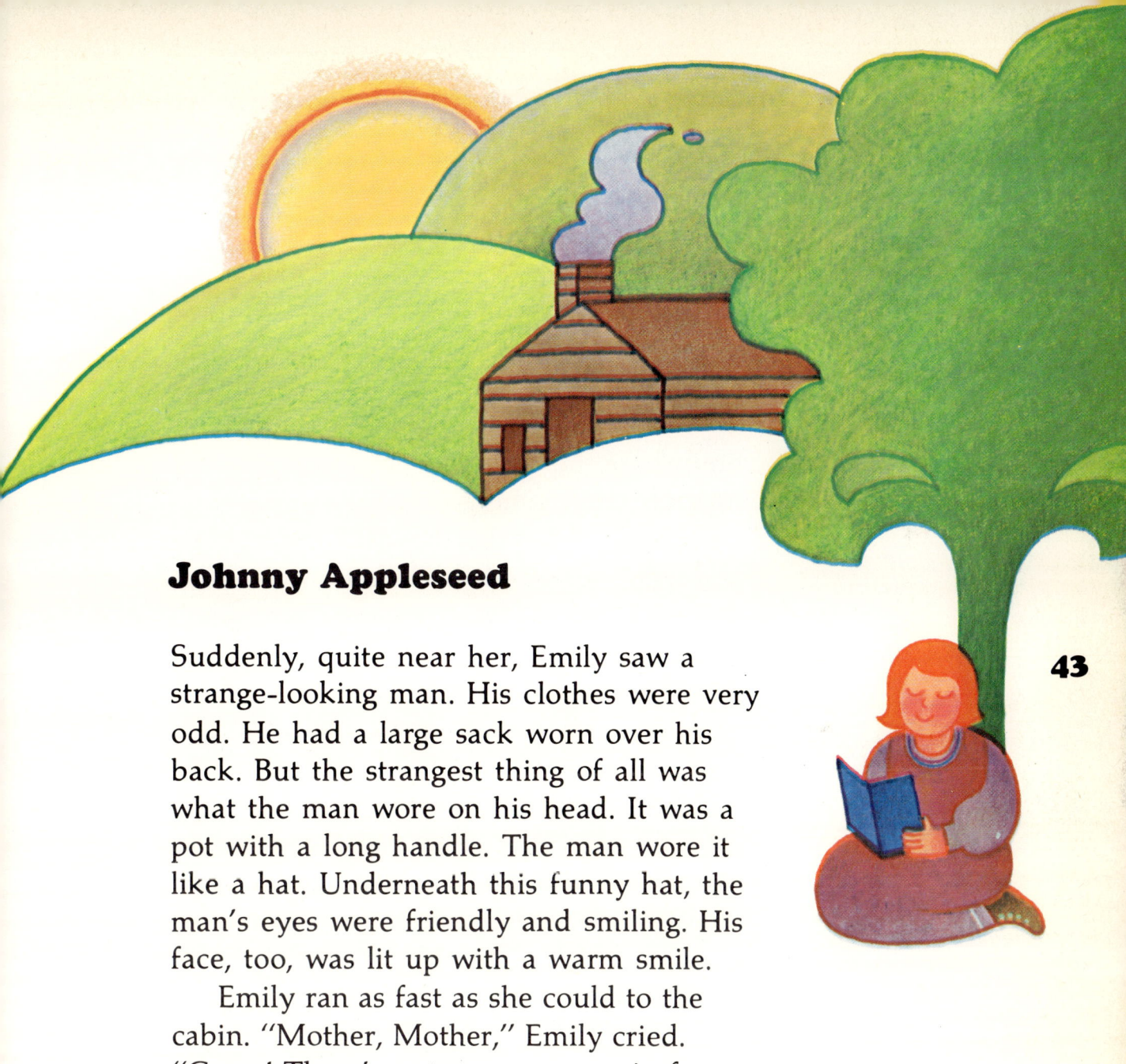

Johnny Appleseed

Suddenly, quite near her, Emily saw a strange-looking man. His clothes were very odd. He had a large sack worn over his back. But the strangest thing of all was what the man wore on his head. It was a pot with a long handle. The man wore it like a hat. Underneath this funny hat, the man's eyes were friendly and smiling. His face, too, was lit up with a warm smile.

Emily ran as fast as she could to the cabin. "Mother, Mother," Emily cried. "Come! There's a stranger, a man in funny clothes. He has a pot on his head!"

"A stranger!" Emily's mother said. "We never see strangers here. Let's go and meet him."

The man was still standing in the clearing. He smiled warmly as Emily and her mother came down the path. Emily's mother went up to the stranger. She held out her hand. "I am Mrs. Worth," she said. "This is my daughter, Emily. Welcome to our home."

The smiling stranger shook hands with Emily's mother. "Thank you, Mrs. Worth," he said. "My name is Johnny Appleseed."

Emily clapped her hands. "Johnny Appleseed!" she shouted. "What a wonderful name!"

"My name is really John Chapman," the man explained. "Everyone calls me Johnny Appleseed because I plant apple trees for people to enjoy."

Then Johnny Appleseed took the sack off his back. He reached into it and brought out a handful of seeds. "If you and your family want me to," Johnny said to Emily's mother, "I will plant an apple orchard here. I will show you how to take care of it."

Emily's head swam. Her heart beat faster. She looked up at her mother with hope in her eyes. Here was her dream come true. In a few years, she would see real apple trees. Emily wanted to hug this new friend. "Johnny Appleseed, you are wonderful!" she cried.

People Grew Happier because of Johnny

Johnny Appleseed believed that all men were God's children. He believed that all men should live together as brothers.

Johnny Appleseed had his own way of helping people. He gave them apples. Apples were food that would help to build strong and healthy bodies. The taste of fresh red apples and the smell of juicy pies cooking made people's lives brighter.

He gave them apple orchards. Now their houses were not just bare cabins. They were more like homes. Strangers passing through often decided not to move on to the wild forests ahead. Instead they decided to settle down near the orchards. Johnny Appleseed's orchards helped to make people live together as neighbors. Many people learned to work and play together as God's children because of Johnny Appleseed.

Stop and Think

Johnny Appleseed did a very good thing for the people. He gave them something as tasty and as beautiful as apples:

1. Can you name some beautiful things in your home, or at school, or at church?

2. What do you do to help keep these things beautiful?

3. Why should you help keep these things beautiful?

Thank Jesus for all beautiful things.

For Home and School

1. There are many stories of Jesus that help us to see how He made other people happy. Can you name some? How did people change because they met or talked to Jesus?

2. Can you think of other people in history who helped people to grow and live in peace?

3. Listen to the evening news with your parents. Tell about anything you heard which makes you think that some people (a) are and (b) are not helping other people to be happy.

7. "Because the Moon Is There!"

The Big Day

It was morning, and everyone was awake and out of bed. The family was gathered around the television set. The children were still in their pajamas. They were sitting on the floor. All eyes were glued to the TV screen. It was a thrilling moment. Men were going to land on the moon.

The adults were silent as they watched. The children were silent, too. Their mouths were wide open. But little Barbara was too young to keep silent very long. She looked away from the TV screen and spoke to her father. "Why, Daddy?" she asked. "Why did the men go to the moon?"

Tommy, Barbara's older brother, spoke before his father had a chance to answer. "Because the moon is *there!*" Tommy shouted. "That's what one of the astronauts said."

Barbara was still looking at her father. Her father smiled at her. "Do you understand?" he asked. Barbara shook her head no. But all the older children shook their heads yes.

Tommy spoke up again. "When I see something—like an island or a lake or a river—I want to go there. I want to see what it's like," he said. "Everyone feels like that. You're the same way, Barbara. When you get a present, you can't wait to open it. You want to see what's inside."

Barbara just buried her head in her father's lap. She did not see what opening presents had to do with going to the moon.

We Like to Know about New Things

But the other children did see. They were old enough to understand why people want to find out everything there is to find out.

Mother wanted to help Barbara understand. She put into words what the older children were really thinking. "God gave us a beautiful world," Mother said. "He wants us to explore it. He wants us to know as much as we can about it. He wants us to know what is in the world and on it and even around it out there in space."

"But why?" Barbara asked. "Why does God want us to know all about the world?"

Mother answered, "God wants us to know because the more we know about the world and everything in it, the more we will know about ourselves."

"You mean, the more I learn about things, the more I grow myself?" Tommy asked.

"That's right," Mother and Father both said together.

We Grow When We Know

"But why do we want to know about the moon?" Barbara asked.

"Because it is part of God's wonderful world," her father said. "God gave us this wonderful world—not only this earth—but all of outer space, too. And he gave us minds, minds that always ask 'Why?' We always want to know more. The more we know, the better people we can be. The more we know about the world and about life, the more we can know about ourselves."

"And about God," Tommy added.

"Yes," his father agreed. "And the more we know, the more we can grow."

"Do we always keep growing—even after we've grown up?" Tommy asked.

Mother and Father both nodded. "Yes," Mother said. "Our minds and our souls never grow old. God wants us to keep on growing and to keep on learning. He wants us to use our knowledge to live better lives. He wants us to love Him and each other. He wants us to live together as His children."

Stop and Think

It is good to want to learn, to ask questions and to want to know more about our world:

1. What is one thing you want to know more about?

2. How can you learn about this thing?

3. Why do you want to learn about it?

Ask Jesus to help you find the right answers to your questions.

For Home and School

1. Talk with your parents about the new discoveries in:

    a. medicine.
    b. space study.
    c. auto safety.

    How do these new discoveries make the world a better place in which to live?

2. Learn this prayer from the Mass:
   "Holy, holy, holy,
   Lord, God of power and might,
   heaven and earth are full of your glory."

2 God's Laws and Ourselves

8. Billy Goes to Visit Strange Worlds

Billy Gets into Trouble

It was one of those days—one of those days when everything went wrong. Billy Moore was mad. Here he was all alone in his room, in bed already, and it wasn't even dark outside.

It had started at breakfast that Saturday morning. Billy's sister, Ruth, said that Billy was old enough to make his own bed and clean up his room.

Billy felt that he was being picked on. He began to argue. Dad got very firm. "No more arguments, Billy," he said. "Make your bed as soon as you've finished breakfast. And pick up your things, too!"

Billy went to his room. He did a very poor job of cleaning it up. Then he raced out of the house before anyone could find anything else for him to do.

Billy called for his friend, Tom, and the two boys decided to play in the park. On the way, they passed Mrs. Ritter's house.

"Let's tease her," Billy said. He walked right to the middle of Mrs. Ritter's lawn and turned a somersault.

Mrs. Ritter rapped angrily on the window. She shouted all sorts of threats. Tom joined in the act. The boys turned somersaults and did handsprings all over the

lawn. Mrs. Ritter grew more and more excited. She rapped harder and harder on the window. She rapped so hard, in fact, that she made a large crack in the window.

Tom and Billy were frightened now. They ran to the park as fast as they could. When they got there, they threw themselves down on the grass. When he found his breath, Tom asked, "Do you think she'll call the police?"

"I don't know," Billy answered. "I just hope she doesn't call my mother and father. I'm in trouble enough as it is."

"It's all your fault anyway," Tom said.

"What do you mean?" Billy shot back. "You were turning somersaults on her lawn, too."

"But you started it!" Tom said. "If I'm in trouble, I'm going to tell my Dad it's your fault."

One word led to another, and the first thing they knew the two boys were fighting, just as though they were enemies instead of friends.

Billy walked home slowly. He had a feeling that there would be more trouble. Sure enough, Billy's mother and father were waiting for him.

"I Wish..."

And so Billy was sent up to bed. He sighed as he lay back on the pillow. He closed his eyes. "I wish I could go someplace where I could do whatever I want to do, whenever I want to do it," he said to himself. "I wish I could live in a place where I wouldn't have to obey my parents. I wish I could live in a place where I didn't have to worry about right and wrong!"

Billy heard a sound. It was a whine, like the noise of a machine or a motor. He opened his eyes. The room was flooded with a strange green light. The light was coming from a big, bright headlight that hung mysteriously, just outside the bedroom window. Billy looked out. He saw a small spaceship hovering in the air. Its engines were throbbing. Its green lights were glowing. As Billy stared in amazement, he heard a voice. "Well, come on, get some clothes on, and hop in," it said.

Billy climbed up on the window sill and jumped through an opening in the side of the spaceship. The door slammed shut. Billy felt a jolt. He fell back as the ship shot forward with a great "whooshing" sound, and soon they were far out in space.

Then, Billy felt a tap on his shoulder. He turned around. There stood a very funny little creature with a pointed head and antennae. "Welcome aboard," said the little creature. "Where to?"

Billy gasped. "What—what—how—why . . .? How should I know?" he finally managed to say.

"You ordered the spaceship," the little fellow replied.

"I did?" Billy asked in wonderment.

"You sure did," the little man said. "Our antennae picked up your thoughts. You wanted to go somewhere where there are no *do's* and *don't's*—right?"

Sam the Spaceman

The little man held out a funny little hand, which Billy shook after a moment's hesitation. "They call me Sam the Spaceman," he said. "I'm at your service. Here, come with me."

Sam went over to a counter and spread out a map. He said to Billy, "Look over this space map and pick your spot."

Billy asked, "What do you mean?"

"Which 'no-rule' place do you want to go to first?" Sam wanted to know. "They're all different."

"Gee—I don't know," Billy said.

"Well, let me help you," Sam said. He pointed to a dot on the map. "This planet is called 'Anything Goes.' There are no parents there, only boys and girls. There is nobody there to give children orders. How would you like to try that?"

"I think I'd like that just fine," Billy said eagerly. "Let's go!"

"Anything Goes, here we come," Sam shouted.

Stop and Think

Billy has just begun a very special adventure. His adventure will help us understand ourselves better:

1. Have you ever been in trouble like Billy? When?

2. What did you do?

3. How did it feel to be in trouble?

Tell Jesus that you are sorry for wrong decisions. Ask Him to help you make the right choices.

For Home and School

1. Learn one of these sayings from the Bible:
   a. "Hatred stirs up fights, but love covers all hurts."
   b. "The hot-headed man makes a fool of himself."
   c. "The patient man shows much good sense."
   Discuss with your parents the one you have learned.

2. Tell ways in which you can be patient:
   a. in school.
   b. at home.
   c. on the playground.

3. Our Father wants us to take care of our things. But He does not want us to think of nothing else. Ask your parents to read to you what Jesus said about this. It is in the Bible (*Matthew 6:25—34*).

9. Anything Goes!

Billy Begins to Learn

The spaceship landed as light as a feather on a grassy hill. The door at the side of the spaceship opened. Billy jumped through it to the ground beneath. Then he picked himself up, dusted himself off, and looked around. There were houses and shops and people everywhere. But the people were all young boys and girls. There were no adults to be seen.

Billy watched the children with great interest. Some were running about here and there. Some were playing games. Others were sitting around looking very bored. They looked, Billy thought, lonely and sad.

"These kids look funny," he said to Sam. "They're so pale and sickly-looking. Some are too fat and some are too thin. They don't look healthy."

"That's because they eat only things like candy and cake," Sam explained. "They don't eat the proper food—the things they need to stay healthy."

"But why doesn't somebody—I mean, why don't their mothers and fathers—?" Billy began. But he stopped. "I forgot," he added. "There are no parents here to tell them what to eat."

Billy walked over to a little girl who was swinging on a gate. "Hello," Billy said to the girl.

"Hello yourself," the little girl said. She stuck her tongue out at Billy.

"Your manners are awful," Billy said.

"What's manners?" the little girl asked.

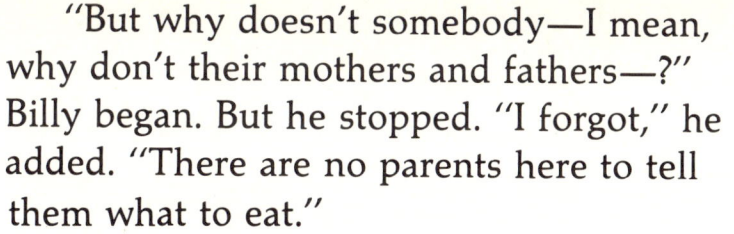

"Didn't anybody ever teach you how to act?" Billy asked.

"Naw," the girl replied. "Nobody taught me."

Where do you go to school?" Billy asked.

"Don't go there," the girl answered. "We got no schools here."

Billy was shocked. "Then you don't even know how to use correct English," he said.

"So what?" the girl said. "Nobody cares how I talk, and I sure don't care. I do what I want."

"But what do you want?" Billy asked.

The little girl stopped swinging. She frowned. She scratched her head and looked puzzled. "You know," she said, "I never thought about that. I don't know what I want."

Do We Need Parents?

"I think I see something I didn't see before," Billy thought to himself. "I see that kids aren't old enough to know what they ought to eat. They aren't old enough to know when to go to bed and get up."

"And how to act and—and lots of things," Sam added. "In other words, let's face it. Boys and girls aren't old enough to be responsible for many things."

"Responsible?" Billy echoed.

"You know," Sam said"—able to do things they *must* do if they are going to grow up to be normal, healthy, interesting human beings."

"So God gave them parents to *help* them grow up right? Is that it?" Billy wondered aloud.

"Sounds right to me," Sam said.

"So it makes sense to obey your parents, after all," Billy thought to himself.

"Well, what do you think?" Sam asked Billy.

"I think these kids don't know what's good for them," Billy said. "I think they need someone who is bigger and wiser to help them."

"To help them? How?" Sam asked.

"Well—to show them, even tell them what to do if they need to be told," Billy answered.

"But who?" Sam wanted to know.

"Someone who cares about them, someone who loves them," Billy said.

"Like parents, maybe?" Sam suggested.

"Yes-s-s," Billy had to admit, "like parents. Who else?"

"Who else is right," Sam said. "Are you saying that kids need parents after all?"

Stop and Think

Billy's adventure isn't going well at all. But he is beginning to see how much he needs the help of others to be good and to grow up:

1. Can you remember a time when you acted badly when no adults were around?

2. What would you do after class today, if no one told you what to do?

3. Why do you do what you are told?

Thank Jesus for all the people who help you grow.

For Home and School

1. Draw a line down the center of a sheet of paper. On one side, make a list of the school subjects that you like. On the other side, make a list of the school subjects that you do not like. Talk with your parents about ways you can improve your work in each of the subjects you listed.

2. Write a short letter to a friend. Tell him or her how people who have good manners bring joy to others:
   a. a mother or a father
   b. a third grade girl or boy
   c. a teacher
   d. a clerk in a store
   Share your letter with your class and with your parents.

3. God gave us our parents to love and guide us. Ask your parents how they guide the different members of the family in different ways.

10. The State of Violence

How to "Settle" Things

With a "whoosh," the spaceship took off again. After the first shuddering thrust into space, the ship sped smoothly on like an arrow.

After the spaceship leveled off, Billy caught his breath. He turned to look around. Sam the Spaceman was at his side once more, waving his antennae in a friendly salute. "Well, friend," Sam said to Billy, "where to now?"

"Somewhere where there are grown-ups as well as kids," Billy replied. "I don't want to see any more of those kids who don't know how to eat or talk right."

"OK," Sam said. "I'll take you to a place where things are really different."

"What is the place called?" Billy asked.

"It's called the 'State of Violence'," Sam answered. "The people there settle everything by fighting. Well, maybe they don't always *settle* everything, but—you'll see."

Billy remembered the bloody nose he had given Tom. That had settled Tom for a while, he thought. "Yes—that might be a good place," Billy said out loud to Sam. "Fighting settles things in a hurry."

Sam gave Billy a wise look. "Well," he said, "you'll see." He sounded almost as if he were talking to himself instead of to Billy.

A short time later the flickering orange lights and a number of buzzers announced that the ship was about to touch down. This time, however, the door in the side of the ship did not open right away. "You've got to be careful here. Someone might be outside looking for a fight," Sam said to Billy.

"Why?" Billy asked in surprise.

"Remember?" Sam asked. "This is the State of Violence. Here they hit first and ask questions afterwards."

The pilot must have looked out and found that no one was around because, suddenly, the door of the spaceship opened. Billy jumped to the ground.

Billy could see four fistfights going on in the street. Grown men were punching each other. One man was pounding another man's head on the pavement. Two women were fighting on a street corner. They were pulling each other's hair and tearing each other's clothes. Two little boys were having their own fight alongside their mothers.

Billy stared at the scene below. "Why doesn't someone stop them?" he finally asked Sam. "Why doesn't a policeman—or—or somebody do something?"

"There are no policemen here," Sam said. "Here they settle everything themselves by fighting."

"See those women?" he went on. "They had an argument over a purse that was on sale in a store. Now they're fighting to see who will buy the purse."

"But why are the two little boys fighting?" Billy wanted to know.

"Their mothers are fighting," Sam explained. "They figure they might as well fight, too."

A Solution?

"It doesn't make any sense!" Billy said.

"They're doing what they want to do," Sam said gently. "Didn't you say that you thought people should do what they feel like doing—not what they are told to do? Didn't you say that fighting was a good way to settle things?" Sam asked.

"I guess I did," Billy said. "But I'm not so sure now."

The sound of shouting reached Billy's ears. He saw a large crowd of big boys. The boys were walking toward the spaceship. "I don't like your looks," one boy shouted at Billy.

"I don't either," another shouted. They were all shouting and shaking their fists at Billy.

"Want to wait around and 'settle things'?" Sam asked Billy.

"Heck no!" Billy shouted.

"I thought you said that fighting settled things?" Sam remarked.

"I've changed my mind," Billy said. "Fighting only causes more trouble."

"It doesn't pay? Is that it?" Sam suggested.

"Yes," Billy answered. "If you can beat up someone else, then someone else can beat you up, too."

"Then everybody gets hurt—right?" Sam said.

"That's right," Billy agreed.

"Want to leave here and go somewhere else?" Sam asked.

"That's for sure!" Billy said. "Let's go!"

With another "whoosh" and lurch, the spaceship shot off on its way.

Stop and Think

The State of Violence was not a very happy place. Billy did not feel good there at all:

1. What happens to you and to others when you fight?

2. Think of some ways to settle things without fighting.

Ask Jesus to help you avoid fighting.

For Home and School

1. Talk about a bully:
   a. Why is he a danger?
   b. How doesn't he control himself?
   c. Why doesn't he act like Jesus?

2. Talk with your parents about how grown-ups have to control their tempers:
   a. at work.
   b. when driving.
   c. at home.

3. Ask your parents how the people in today's news:
   a. showed patience with others.
   b. were not patient with others.

11. Crooksville

Take What You Want

The spaceship raced on through the heavens like a shooting star. Billy sat back in his seat. He was glad to be safe inside the ship, far away from the angry crowds in the State of Violence.

"Well, my friend, what's next on your list of places?" Sam said to Billy.

"Gee, I don't know," Billy answered. "I didn't like the places we've seen so far."

"Well," Sam said, rubbing his funny little chin. "We could try Crooksville. It's a place where anybody is allowed to take anything he can get away with. Stealing is all right there if you are big enough to get away with it."

"That would be nice," Billy said. "I need some new things, especially a bike."

When the spaceship landed, it settled down on the roof of a tall building in the center of town. Billy was excited. This would be a new adventure, he was sure.

A Crook in Crooksville

The first thing Billy saw in the street was a new bicycle parked against a building. It was not chained. It was just standing there ready to be taken. "This is too good to be true," Billy thought. He jumped on the bicycle and pedaled down the street.

After riding around for a while, Billy felt very hot. "It would be nice to find a swimming pool," he thought. And soon he did find a swimming pool. At the entrance there was a sign that said "Swimming Trunks for Rent—50¢."

"I don't see how I can steal a pair of trunks," Billy thought. But he had four quarters in his pocket. He took them out. He placed two quarters on the counter and got a pair of trunks. He was about to put the other two quarters back in his pocket when a big boy grabbed his hand. The boy took the quarters before Billy knew what was happening.

Billy wanted to call a policeman. Then he remembered, "This is Crooksville." He sighed.

Billy went into the locker room. As he took off his clothes, he laid them carefully on the bench beside him. He put on the swimming trunks, keeping his eyes on his clothes all the time. He knew he would have to leave his clothes with the man in charge of the locker room. They would not be safe otherwise. He saw a basket for clothes just a few yards away.

Billy walked over and picked up the basket. He turned his back on the bench for only a minute. He walked only a few steps away. But when Billy returned to the bench, his clothes were gone. Someone had helped himself to everything Billy was wearing. When Billy left the pool, he found that the bicycle he was riding had been stolen, too.

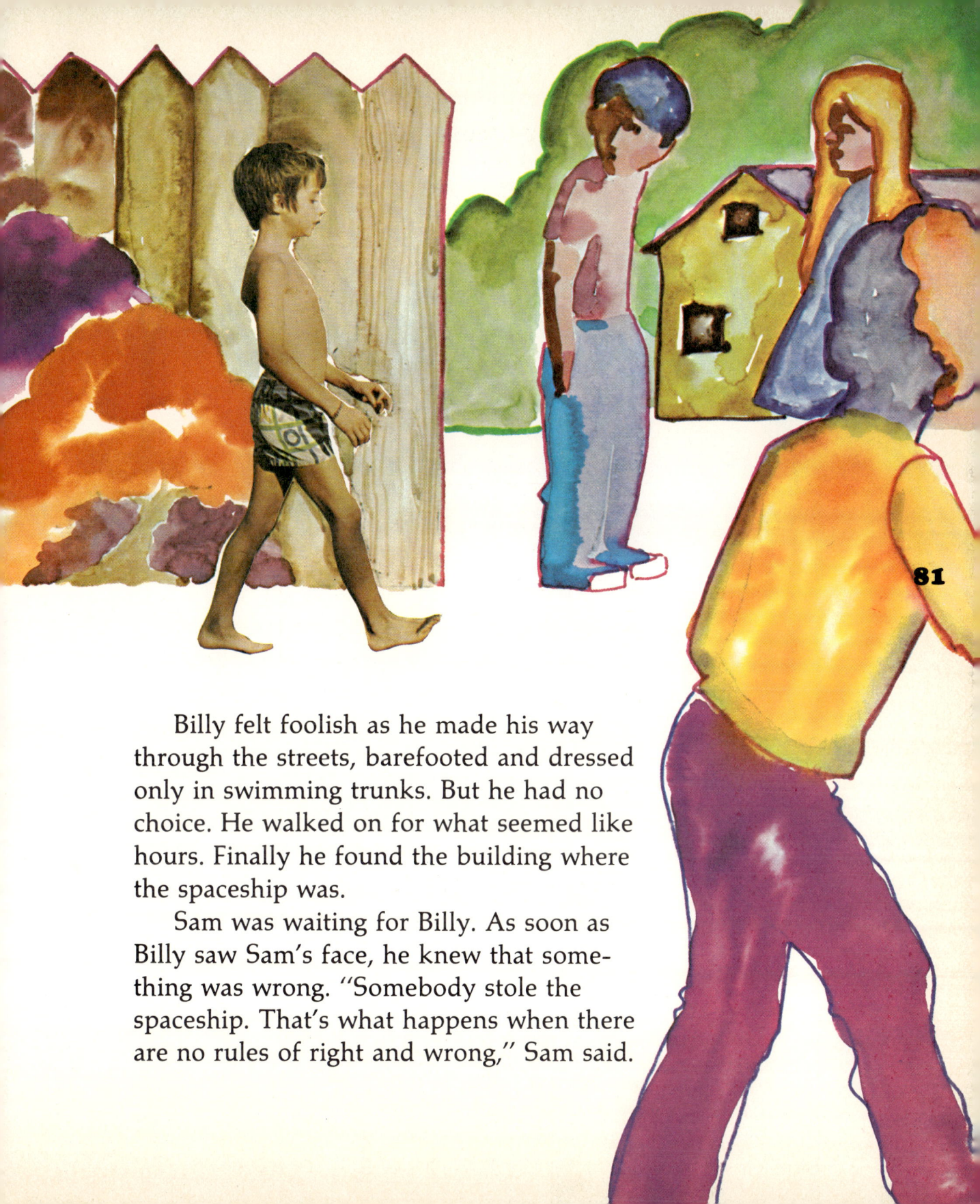

Billy felt foolish as he made his way through the streets, barefooted and dressed only in swimming trunks. But he had no choice. He walked on for what seemed like hours. Finally he found the building where the spaceship was.

Sam was waiting for Billy. As soon as Billy saw Sam's face, he knew that something was wrong. "Somebody stole the spaceship. That's what happens when there are no rules of right and wrong," Sam said.

"How do we get out of here?" Billy asked.

"I've radioed for another spaceship," Sam said. "We'd better stay right here and wait. It may be days."

So Billy and Sam sat there for three days. It was cold at night. Billy was hot sitting in the sun all day. He was thirsty, and above all he was hungry. But more than anything else, he was anxious to get away—to go someplace, any place. "I've had enough of Crooksville," Billy told Sam. "I want to go somewhere where people are honest, even if I have to be honest myself!"

Sam said, "Good! I think I see the spaceship coming."

Stop and Think

Crooksville was not a good place, either. It is very hard to live when people steal what we have:

1. How do you feel when someone takes something from you?

2. How do you think others feel when you take things from them?

3. Why do you think we have laws against stealing?

Ask Jesus to help you respect the property of others.

For Home and School

1. Talk about whether the following things are more important than people:
   - a. money
   - b. party clothes
   - c. new house
   - d. many friends

2. Ask your parents to tell you how the following people need courage so that they will not steal:
   - a. clerk in a store
   - b. person working a cash register
   - c. businessman
   - d. salesman
   - e. mechanic in a gas station

12. The Land of Try Anything Once

The Crazy Bus Ride

The spaceship landed in an open field this time. When Billy climbed out, he saw a highway just a few yards away. There was a bus stop at the corner. Billy decided to take a bus and ride into town. In a little while, a bus came along. It was going much too fast, Billy thought. It screeched to a stop and Billy got on.

As soon as the bus started up again, Billy wished he had decided to walk to town instead. The driver had a crazy look on his face. His eyes were glassy. He wore a silly grin. But, worst of all, he drove the bus like a madman. Most of the passengers had the same silly grin and glassy eyes. They actually seemed to be enjoying the crazy ride.

A boy who was sitting in the seat next to Billy poked him in the ribs. "Some driver, eh kid?" he said. "He's on speed!"

"What do you mean?" Billy asked.

"Pep pills!" the boy cried. "They're the greatest! I'm on them, too!" The boy reached into his pocket and pulled out a handful of pills. "Here, like to try a few? They'll make you high, high, high!"

"But maybe I don't want to get that high," Billy told him.

"Then you take a 'downer,'" the boy replied, "one of these blue ones, or one of these red ones." He held out some sleeping pills.

"Gee, I don't—" Billy began, but he never finished. The bus crashed into a tree. The driver slumped over the wheel. The passengers fell forward. Someone opened the door, and Billy rushed out. He ran down the road. He wanted to get far away from the crazy bus and the strange people.

How *Not* to Drive a Car

A car was coming along the highway. Billy gave the hitchhiker sign. The driver jammed on the brakes, and the car stopped right next to Billy. A girl about his own age was driving. "Hop in," the girl said.

Billy climbed into the front seat. "Boy," he said to the young driver, "this is neat. How come they let you drive a car?"

"Well," the girl said, "they don't *let* me exactly. This is my father's car. I decided I'd try anything once. I've always wanted to drive a car." She put the car in gear. With a great lurch, it jumped ahead and began to speed down the highway.

The girl seemed confused and sort of scared. She turned and looked at Billy. "I'm not sure I know how to drive this thing yet," she admitted.

"Hey!" Billy yelled. "Keep your eyes on the road!"

But it was too late. With a horrible crash the car smashed into a truck that was parked by the side of the road. The car was a total wreck. But, by some miracle, neither Billy nor the girl seemed to be hurt.

The girl began to cry. "What will my father say?" she moaned.

"Well," Billy said, "you tried something once, didn't you? You'll try something else when you tell your father."

Come on, Light Up!

Billy left the girl and began walking along the side of the road again. Soon, he noticed a group of boys down the road. They were all smoking cigarettes. One boy called to him, "Come on, have a smoke."

Billy replied, "Sure, I'll try anything once." Billy took the cigarette. He put it to his lips. He sucked the smoke deep into his lungs. Suddenly, Billy choked. He coughed. He sputtered. He grew red in the face. He felt as if he were going to die right there on the spot.

"He's chicken!" one of the boys said. "He doesn't know how to smoke." But even as he said these words, the boy got a bad fit of coughing himself.

"I'll show them!" Billy thought. He took another deep drag on the cigarette. Once again, he choked and sputtered and coughed. Now he began to feel really sick.

All of a sudden Billy didn't care what the other boys thought. He handed the cigarette back to the boy who had given it to him. "See ya," Billy said as he stumbled along the road. He felt sick and dizzy and miserable.

Let's Get Going!

Billy started to walk back to the place where the spaceship had landed. As he passed the wrecked bus, Billy met the boy he had talked to on the bus. The boy looked different. The "high" he had gotten from his pills had worn off. He was so worn out and tired-looking that Billy thought he was almost unconscious. He lay on the grass and sighed and rolled his eyes.

"They're all sick! They all feel terrible!" Billy said. "These people must be crazy to take pills like this."

Sam was waiting for Billy at the spaceship. "Well," Sam said, "what do you think of Try Anything Once?"

"I don't know," Billy said. "I tried a couple of things, but so far I haven't really had any fun."

"You want to get going?" Sam asked.

"Heck, yes!" Billy shouted. "Let's go!"

Stop and Think

Some people will try anything. But many things just can't be tried without having some bad effects on our health or safety:

1. Can you remember a time when you did not follow health or safety rules? What happened?

2. What have you seen happen to other people when they did not follow the rules?

3. Think of times when you tried new things. How were some of these things good? How were some of them bad?

Ask Jesus to give you the courage to do what has to be done. Ask Him, too, to help you know what new things would be bad for you.

For Home and School

1. Make a collage of magazine pictures which shows people doing things for the first time. Share it with your class and your parents.

2. It is easy for us to cause accidents when we are careless, or when we do not know about what we are using. Discuss in class what we learn from the following subjects:
   a. accident prevention
   b. first aid
   c. driver safety
   d. drug, alcohol, and tobacco abuse
   e. swimming safety

3. Make a list of things you would like to try once. Include things that you can do now, and things that you will be able to do when you are older. Discuss your list with your parents.

13. Billy Comes Back to Earth

At Home Again

Billy settled back in his seat in the spaceship and closed his eyes. Suddenly he heard a sound, a loud shrieking sound. "It's a fire engine," Billy thought to himself,

Billy sat up and opened his eyes. He was in his own room.

The Ten Commandments

At breakfast the next day, Billy told his dream to the family. "Those places certainly were funny!" Billy said. Then he asked his mother and father, "Do people act like that in real life?"

"Some do and some don't," his mother said.

"If they do, they should be locked up!" Billy cried. "They hurt themselves. They hurt me. They're crazy."

His father said, "Maybe you're ready now to understand more about the Commandments of God."

Billy cut in, "You mean the Ten Commandments? I know them! I can say them!"

"That's right," his father replied. "But do you see that they are meant to help people? People who live by the Commandments don't do crazy things like the people in your dream."

"Do you know where we got them? The Commandments, I mean," asked Billy's sister, Ruth.

"Sure I do," Billy said proudly. "God gave them to Moses. Then Moses gave them to the Israelites, God's chosen People."

"That's right," Ruth said. "But now *I've* got a question." Everyone turned and looked at Ruth. "Was this new news to the people—what Moses told them?"

"That's a very good question, Ruth. What do *you* think?" her mother asked.

"I think they *must* have known," Ruth answered.

"You're right," her father said. "These things are sort of written in our hearts by God."

"But, then, why would God have to tell Moses to give these Commandments to the people?" Billy wanted to know.

"Do you suppose," his mother asked, "that God wanted the people to know these laws come from *Him*?"

"That's right!" Ruth said brightly. "The people always knew it was wrong to lie and steal. But now they knew why. They knew that God was—*behind* these Commandments."

"Why don't we all talk about this when we have lots of time?" their mother suggested. "How about tonight after supper?"

"OK," Billy said. "Now I've got to see Tommy and Mrs. Ritter. I think I'd better get some things over with before tonight."

Stop and Think

God has given us some good rules to live by. These rules are called Commandments:

1. What are some rules your parents have made for you?

2. Why do your parents make rules for you?

3. What do you know about the Commandments God has given us?

Ask Jesus to help you always live by God's Commandments.

For Home and School

1. Give some examples of things you did when you were young which you would not do now. Why wouldn't you do them now?

2. Even though the Commandments are written in our hearts, God wanted us to know that they came from Him. That is why He gave them to Moses. Discuss with your parents why God wanted us to know the Commandments came from Him.

14. "Love God with Your Whole Heart"

God Gives Moses the Commandments

"First, I'll read from the nineteenth chapter of the Book of Exodus," Billy's father told the family. "Then we'll read about the Ten Commandments in the twentieth chapter."

Billy's mother and the three children sat in silence while Dad opened the Bible, found the page, and began to read. They listened with great attention as they heard how Moses went up the mountain and spoke with God:

> Then Moses led the people out of the camp to meet God; and they stood at the bottom of the mountain. The mountain of Sinai was all wrapped in smoke, for the Lord came upon it in fire. Like smoke from a furnace the smoke went up, and the whole mountain shook violently. Louder and louder grew the

sound of a trumpet. Moses spoke and God answered him, and peals of thunder sounded. The Lord came down to the top of the mountain of Sinai, and He called Moses to the top of the mountain, and Moses went up to Him.

"That is the way the Bible tells us about the meeting between God and Moses," Billy's father said. "Now I'll read you the Commandments." He went on reading:

Then God spoke all these commandments: "I, the Lord, am your God, who brought you out of the land of Egypt, that place of slavery.

"You shall have no other gods besides me.

"You shall not take the name of the Lord, your God, in vain.

"Remember to keep holy the sabbath day.

"Honor your father and your mother.

"You shall not kill.

"You shall not commit adultery.

"You shall not steal.

"You shall not bear false witness against your neighbor.

"You shall not covet your neighbor's house.

"You shall not covet your neighbor's wife, not his male or female slave, nor his ox, or his ass, nor anything else that belongs to him."

The First Three Commandments

Billy's father closed the Bible. "Now I have a question," he said. "What do these Commandments of God tell us?"

Ruth spoke up. "They tell us how we are supposed to act as human beings and children of God," she said.

Billy broke in. "They tell us what is right and wrong," he said.

"You are both right," their mother said. "God made us. We are His children. We depend on Him for everything. Some of these Commandments tell us that we must worship God and have respect for His name."

"Those are the first two!" Billy shouted.

"Right again!" his mother said. "Now, what about the third, the one about the Sabbath?"

"That's a special one," Ruth said. "Other people didn't know about that one. Only God's People, the Israelites, knew."

"And we keep Sunday as our holy day now instead of the Sabbath," Billy added.

Billy's father seemed proud of the answers the children had given. "That's right," he said. "The first three Commandments tell us how to show our love for God."

Stop and Think

The first three Commandments help us to know what God wants us to do. They help us to love God and worship Him:

1. Can you remember the first three Commandments by heart?

2. Why do you think we need to pray?

3. How does God help us day-by-day in all that we do?

Tell God how much you love Him.

For Home and School

1. Get together in small groups. Within the groups, talk about how the first three Commandments help us to grow as Christian boys and girls.

2. Collect pictures of people worshipping God in church. Talk about the different ways in which we, as Catholics, worship God.

3. Make up a prayer to God in which you promise to love Him more. Perhaps your parents can help you.

15. "Love Your Neighbor as Yourself"

The Commandments Help Us Live in Peace

Billy and his family were still talking about the Commandments. "We talked about the first three," Billy's father said. "Now, how about the other seven Commandments. What do they tell us?"

This time both Ruth and Billy were silent. They weren't sure they knew the answer. Larry hadn't said a word up to now. He figured that now he'd say *something*. "I give up," Larry said. "What do they tell us?"

Mother cut in. "Well," she said, "let's try to figure it out. The first three Commandments tell us how we must act towards God. What do you suppose the others would tell us?"

Ruth's face lit up. "Oh, I think I know!" she cried. "Do they tell us how we must act towards other people?"

"That's right!" her mother said, smiling. "They tell us how we must act towards ourselves and towards everyone else."

"We are all God's children," their father added. "In His Commandments God spells out how we must respect each person's rights and live together as His children."

"So God tells us that we hurt others if we lie to them, or steal from them, or fight with them, or spread stories about them—and things like that," Ruth said.

"Yes," her mother said. "If we do things like that, we are acting against love of our neighbor."

"And that means we are acting against our love of God, too, doesn't it?" Ruth asked.

"That's right," her father said. "If we don't love God's children, we aren't loving God."

Billy's Idea

Everyone was silent for a moment. Then Billy had a bright idea. He spoke up. "Hey! I just thought of something!" he said. "These Commandments tell us what we shouldn't do against other people, don't they—like lying and stealing and fighting and hating?"

Everyone nodded yes and waited.

"Well, then," Billy went on, "they tell everyone else what they shouldn't do to *me*! Right?"

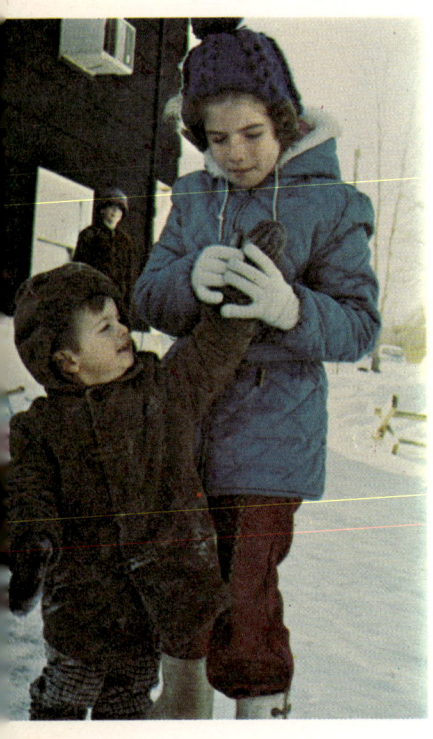

"That's right," Mother and Dad said together.

"Then the Commandments work for me," Billy cried. "They help me! They keep people from hurting me!"

Mother and Dad agreed again.

"Gee!" Billy said. "I dreamed all about that. I should have realized."

"You know," Ruth said, "I always thought of the Commandments as something God gave us to *test* us."

"But that isn't so, is it?" her mother put in.

"No—not at all," Ruth said. "God told us about the Commandments to *protect* us from ourselves. He wanted us to be happy."

"You've got it right, Ruth," her father said. "God wants us to be happy. He told us about the Commandments to help us love Him and others more, to respect each other's rights, and live together in peace."

Billy spoke up again. "We shouldn't think of God as a scorekeeper or a policeman, then," he said.

"No, I should say not," his mother said. "God loves you all even more than we do. We should always think of Him as He really is—as our Father."

Stop and Think

The last seven Commandments tell us how we should treat other people. They help us show people how much we love them, and want to live peacefully with them:

1. Can you remember the last seven Commandments by heart?

2. Think of a time when you wanted to be mean to someone, or maybe wanted to take something that did not belong to you. Did you think about God's Commandments?

3. How can these Commandments help us love other people?

Ask Jesus to help you be kind and caring for others.

For Home and School

1. Get together in small groups. Within the groups, talk about how the last seven Commandments help us grow as Christian boys and girls.

2. On a large piece of cardboard, print the Ten Commandments. Hang up your work in a special place in your room so that you can see it frequently.

3. Ask your parents to read to you how Jesus summed up the Ten Commandments *(Matthew 22:36—40)*. Discuss with your parents.

16. "I Think You're Beginning to Grow Up"

There Are Other Reasons

"You know, Ruth, I liked what you said," Billy told his sister. Ruth took a bite of her cookie and looked at Billy. She was pleased. It wasn't very often that her younger brother said something nice to her. "I mean," Billy went on, "what you said about how God's Commandments help us."

Ruth nodded. "Yes. I didn't always know that. I used to think the Commandments were just hard old rules we had to obey or *else*."

"That's what I mean," Billy said. "I think I see now that there are other reasons."

"Like when Dad told me I had to clean up my room," Billy went on. "I didn't want to. I only did it because I knew I'd be punished if I didn't. Now I think I see another reason why I should have done what Dad said."

"What's the other reason?" Ruth asked.

"To please Mom, and Dad," Billy answered, "to make them feel good—you know, so they'd be—well—proud of me."

Ruth took another sip of her milk. She looked very thoughtful for a minute. Then she grinned at Billy. "You know something?" she said. "I think you're beginning to grow up."

"Little kids don't think like that," Ruth went on. "They seldom do things because they want to please other people, or want to please God even. They do things because they know they'll be clobbered if they don't."

"Like him," Billy said, pointing to his little brother, Larry. "He's like Queenie. He doesn't know right from wrong. He's good only because he's afraid he'll be punished if he isn't."

"I Know It Hurts You"

Larry banged his glass on the table. "I'm not like Queenie!" he said angrily. "Queenie is dumb. She can't think or talk. You're teasing me again. I'm gonna tell Dad, and he'll clobber *you!*"

"See what I mean?" Billy said. "He's just a baby. All he thinks of is that if he does something wrong, he'll be clobbered."

"But you still tease him and you're not supposed to," Ruth pointed out. "I used to tease Larry a lot," she said. "But I don't do it so much any more. You know why?"

Billy was thinking, but he waited for Ruth to answer her own question.

Larry cut in. " 'Cause you'd be clobbered, too," he shouted at Ruth.

"No," Ruth said. "I used to feel that way. But do you know why I try not to tease you now?"

"Why?" Larry demanded.

"Because I know it hurts you when I tease you," Ruth told him.

Billy was silent for a while. he was thinking deeply. "You know," he said finally, "I went over to Mrs. Ritter's yesterday. I told her I was sorry I turned somersaults on her lawn."

"Gee, Billy, I'm glad you did that!" Ruth said.

"Yeah," Billy went on. "At first, I was sorry just because I knew I'd get it from Mom and Dad. But later, I was sorry because I made Mrs. Ritter feel bad."

"I told you that you were beginning to grow up," Ruth said.

"You think you're so smart!" Larry said to his brother.

Billy was about to snap back at Larry. But he stopped for a minute. Then he grinned at his little brother instead. Playfully, he poked Larry in the ribs. He said, "You'll be smart yourself someday, kid. All you have to do is grow up a little."

Stop and Think

There are many reasons for doing good things. Billy told us about some of them:

1. Can you give some more reasons for doing good things?

2. What are some good things that you do for others?

3. Why do you do them?

Ask Jesus to help you **know** why you do the things you do.

For Home and School

1. As we grow up, we begin to look at things we do in a way different from when we were younger. Discuss how you looked upon the following things then, and now:
    a. cleaning your room
    b. helping around the house
    c. making friends
    d. obeying your parents and other grown-ups

2. Ask your parents how they feel when you do kind things for them and others.

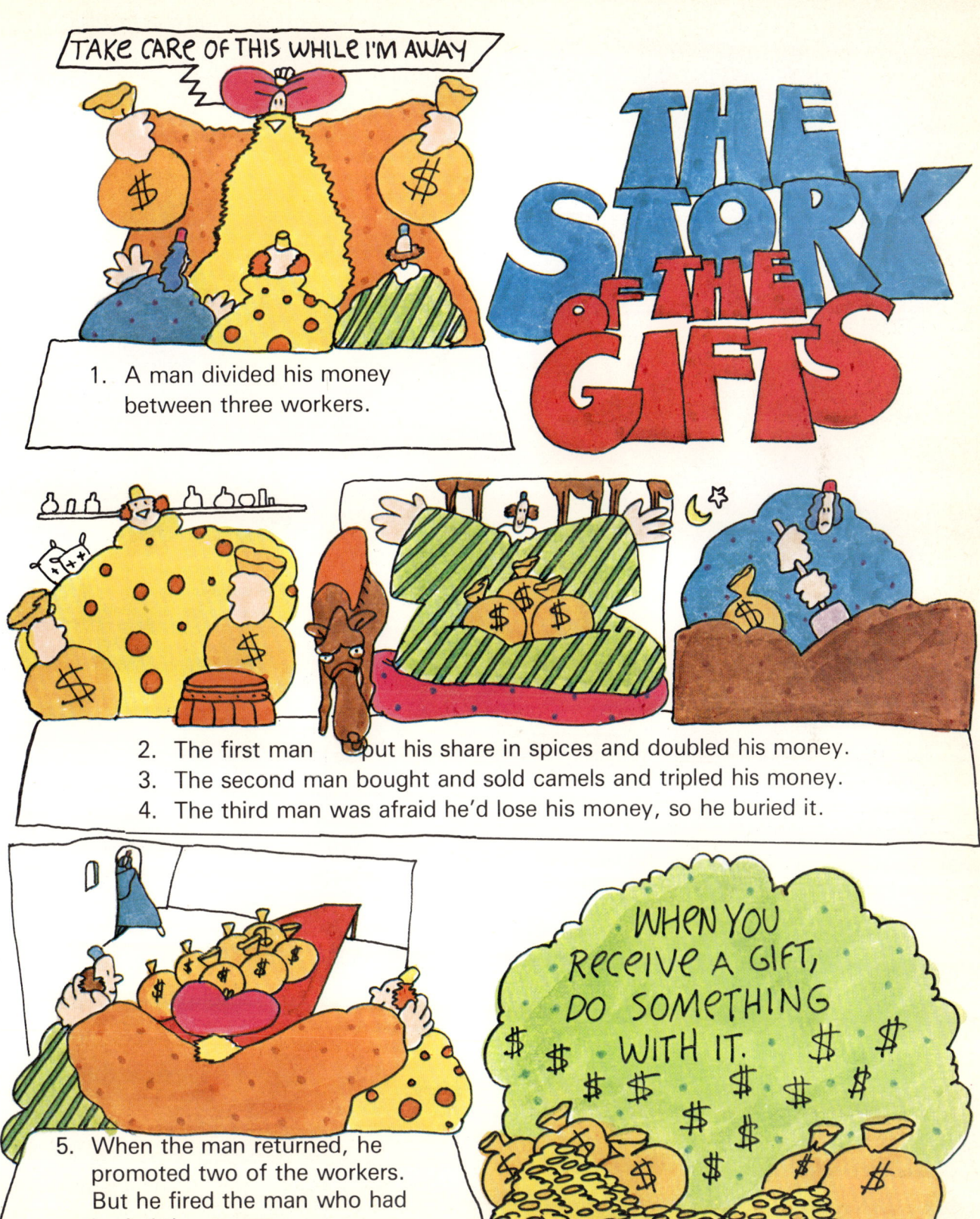

3 We Are Led by God

17. Let Your Conscience Be Your Guide

Pinocchio Learned

"I don't care about anything. I just want to have fun." This is what Pinocchio said when he first came alive and found out that he could move and talk.

Pinocchio, the wooden puppet, did not care about how other people felt. He did not care what happened to them. He never stopped to think about how others would suffer because of what he did.

So Pinocchio ran away from school. He wandered off and got lost. He never even thought about how his father, the toy-maker, would worry about him. He never thought that his father would leave the toy shop and go searching for him.

Pinocchio didn't bother about the Fairy with the Blue Hair either. He didn't think about how she would suffer because of him. He didn't know or care that she would feel so sad about what he did.

But then something happened to Pinocchio. He began to listen to his conscience. His conscience told him that he hurt his father by running away. It let him know how the Fairy with the Blue Hair suffered because he was so selfish.

Pinocchio listened to his conscience. He began to think about what was right and wrong. He learned that when he did things that were right, he pleased those who loved him. He learned that when he did things that were wrong, he caused those who loved him to suffer.

Pinocchio listened to his conscience. He realized that he *wanted* to please those who loved him. He realized that he did not want others to suffer because of what he did or did not do. Pinocchio got a great reward when he listened to his conscience and obeyed it. He became a real boy.

All boys and girls are something like Pinocchio. At first, when they are little children, they do only what they feel like doing. They don't know right from wrong, really. They do things or do not do things only because they don't want to be punished. They do not yet know that other people are happy or sad because of what they do.

But when boys and girls grow a little older, they begin to realize that if they do what is right, they will please God and their parents and others who love them. They begin to develop a conscience about their actions. They begin to want to please God and their parents and other people.

Everyone Has a Conscience

God gives every person a conscience. By listening to their consciences, people know what is right and what is wrong. They know what is good and pleasing to God. They know what is sinful, and not pleasing to God, too.

God even *teaches* people so that they will know what is right and wrong. He speaks to them in many ways.

God spoke to His people many, many years ago through Moses. Moses was a great leader whom God chose to lead His People. God gave Moses the Ten Commandments. When the people listened to Moses about the Commandments, they were listening to God. When they did what their consciences told them and obeyed these Commandments, they knew that they were pleasing God. When they disobeyed these Commandments, they knew that they were sinning against the God who loved them so much.

God still speaks to His People today. First, He speaks through His Son, Jesus Christ. Jesus speaks to everyone. But Jesus does much more than just tell people what to do. He *shows* people how to act. He shows them how to please God our Father. And He shows them how to love one another.

God also speaks to His People today through His Church. He speaks through the Pope, bishops, and priests. Through them, God reminds us of the Ten Commandments He gave to His people long ago.

Finally, God speaks to boys and girls in a special way. He speaks to them through their parents, teachers, and other adults. Children know that they please God when they obey their elders. They know that they please God by keeping His Commandments. They try to obey the Commandments and not sin against God and their neighbor.

Stop and Think

When Pinocchio learned to listen to his conscience, he found out that he **wanted** to please those who loved him:

1. How do we know what God wants us to do?

2. When we know that what we do is good, what should we do?

3. When we learn that something we want to do is against God's rules, what should we do?

Promise Jesus that you will try to live by what you know is right.

For Home and School

1. Look up the word "conscience" in the dictionary. What does it mean? Discuss its meaning with your class and your parents.

2. Name some examples of how God teaches us today through:
    a. Jesus.
    b. the Church.
    c. parents and other adults.

18. "Honor Your Father and Your Mother"

We Grow through Help and Love

As soon as Janet came in the back door, she could feel excitement in the air.

The baby was standing on her feet. She was holding on to Dad's hands. But the baby was looking at her mother. Her mother's smiling eyes were coaxing her. Her mother's voice was calling her. Her mother's arms were inviting the baby to walk over to her mother all by herself.

The baby was afraid. Her mother was only a few feet away. But to the baby it seemed like a long, long way. Still, her mother's eyes were warm. Her mother's voice was full of love. Her mother's arms were coaxing her. All at once, the baby's face broke into a big smile. She forgot her fears. She pushed herself forward toward her mother's waiting arms. One—two—three—four steps—all by herself. And there she was in her mother's arms!

Parents Lead Little by Little

Later that night, Janet thought about the baby's first steps. The next day, she talked about it with her mother. "Mom, you had to coax Margie to walk, didn't you?" Janet asked.

"Yes," her mother replied. "I had to give the baby confidence. I had to make her want to walk. I had to make her feel that she *could* walk. So I held out my arms and called to her."

Janet was thinking very fast now. "That's true about a lot of things, isn't it?" she asked. "I mean, not just walking, but everything?"

"That's right," Janet's mother said. "Mothers and fathers lead their children little by little. We help you talk and walk and learn and grow day by day."

That night as Janet was about to say "God bless Mom and Dad," she stopped and thought again. "God gave me a mother and father to help me be what I want to be. And they also help me be what God wants me to be," Janet thought.

Janet's thoughts went on. "My Mother and Father know much more than I know. They know what is good for me. They want me to be happy. They love me. They want me to grow up to be good."

"I think I know better now why I should obey Mom and Dad," Janet said to herself. "I think I understand why I respect them and love them."

Finally Janet said to God, "Please bless Mom and Dad." She really meant it.

Stop and Think

Mothers and fathers are special gifts to us from God:

1. What are some of the things we have learned from our parents?

2. What are some things our parents ask us to do?

3. Are we ever afraid to do them?

4. What are some reasons for obeying our parents?

Ask Jesus to bless and care for your parents.

For Home and School

1. Make a list of things which your family does to help you. Be sure to thank them for loving you and doing good things for you.

2. Write your own poem which tells how you can show your love for your family. Give the poem to your parents.

3. Some boys and girls cause their parents to lose their tempers. Talk about the things Christian boys and girls can do to help make their homes peaceful.

19. Together We Are Strong

Parents Teach Us to Work Together

Parents love their children. They want them to be healthy and happy. They want them to do what is right. Parents teach their children how to act.

Sometimes, parents teach their children by showing them what to do. A mother sets the table while her little girl watches. Then the little girl tries to set the table just as her mother did.

Sometimes, parents teach their children by telling them what to do. They say over and over again, "Brush your teeth," "Pick up your clothes," "Let the dog out." By doing what he is told, a child learns how to act.

Sometimes, too, parents teach their children by telling them stories. Here is a story about working together.

The Body

Once upon a time, several parts of the human body got together and held a meeting. The hands, feet, eyes, nose, and mouth got together to talk about the stomach. They were angry with the stomach.

The hands rapped on the desk to open the meeting. The eyes spoke up first. "We see the food on the table, and it looks so good. But the stomach gets it all."

"That's right," the nose agreed. "I smell the wonderful food, but that is all I have a chance to do."

The mouth had its say, too. "I chew the food. I even get to taste it. But the food still goes to the stomach."

The hands and feet shouted together, "That's right! It just isn't fair."

So all the parts of the body decided to go on strike against the stomach.

"We won't reach for it and put it into the mouth," the hands promised.

"Don't worry," the feet said. "We won't even let the stomach get near the food."

Days passed. Strange things started to happen. The legs and feet were too weak to walk. The arms and hands could barely reach out. The mouth was dry.

Only then did these parts of the body understand a great truth. Now they realized that the stomach did not take the food just for itself. The stomach helped the whole body. It changed the food into nourishment for each part of the body.

The parts of the body learned that they are all part of one body. They saw that they all must work together. When they did not work together, the whole body suffered. When they did not help each other, every part was hurt.

The Farmer

Once upon a time there lived an old farmer. The farmer had seven sons. The sons were always fighting about who would do the work around the farm.

One day, the father became sick. The old man knew that he was soon going to die. He was very worried about his sons. How would they ever get along after he was gone? The old man began to pray. Then suddenly, he had an idea.

He called his seven sons. "Come to my bedside tonight after supper," he said. "Each one of you bring a stick. I want to teach you all a lesson."

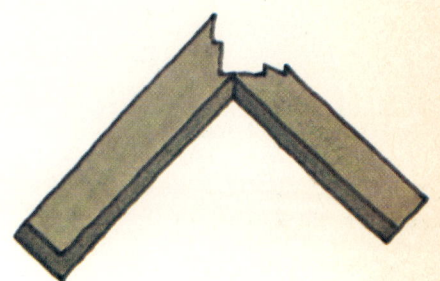

That night, the seven brothers gathered around their father's bed. Each brother had a stick. "Give me your sticks, one at a time," the old man said. In turn, each son handed his father a stick. The old man took each stick in his hands. With one flick of his wrists, he broke each one in half.

"You see," he said, "I am old and weak. Yet one by one, even I can break each stick."

Then the old farmer reached under his pillow. He brought out seven more sticks.

The father tied the sticks together with a piece of string. "Now," said the old man, "take this bundle of sticks. Try to break it in half with your bare hands."

The oldest son took the sticks from his father. With all his might he tried to break the bundle. He could not. And so it was with all the brothers. Each one tried. None was able to break the bundle.

Then the father said, "I have tried to teach you a lesson. I am old and weak. But when I took your sticks, one by one, I had no trouble breaking them. You are young and strong. But when seven sticks were tied together in one bundle, even you could not break them. I hope you will remember this always."

Stop and Think

The bundle of sticks was so much stronger than the single one. The body worked so much better when the parts were not fighting among themselves:

1. Can you remember a time when you found working together on something to be a good thing?

2. Can you think of some good things about yourself which could help others?

3. Can you think of some things you need from others that would help you to work better?

Ask Jesus to help you see the reasons for working together.

For Home and School

1. Discuss in class the saying, "Many hands make light work."

2. Make up a story about a country in which none of the citizens want to help each other. Remember to tell what would happen in the country?

3. Share with the class your memories of a time when you and your family had a party. What did each member of the family do to help make the meal a success?

20. The Tongue Is a Gift from God

Parents Teach Us How to Use Our Speech

When we were small, our parents taught us to say words. Now, they help us by teaching us correct English. But our parents also teach us how to *use* our speech. People can use their tongues in good or bad ways. Our parents teach us to tell the truth. They teach us not to lie.

Sometimes parents teach their children this lesson by telling them stories.

The Foolish Donkey

There is a very short story about a very foolish donkey. He tried to be something he was not. He gave himself away when he opened his mouth. The story also tells us something important about the way we use our tongues.

Once upon a time, a donkey found a lion skin. He put the skin on. Then he walked among the other animals. He frightened the animals. All except the fox were afraid. The fox was doubtful.

The donkey tried to frighten the fox. He opened his mouth to roar like a lion. But all that came out was the silly "hee-haw" of a donkey.

The fox and all the other animals laughed. The donkey was ashamed. "I might have been frightened, too," the fox said. "You should have kept your mouth shut."

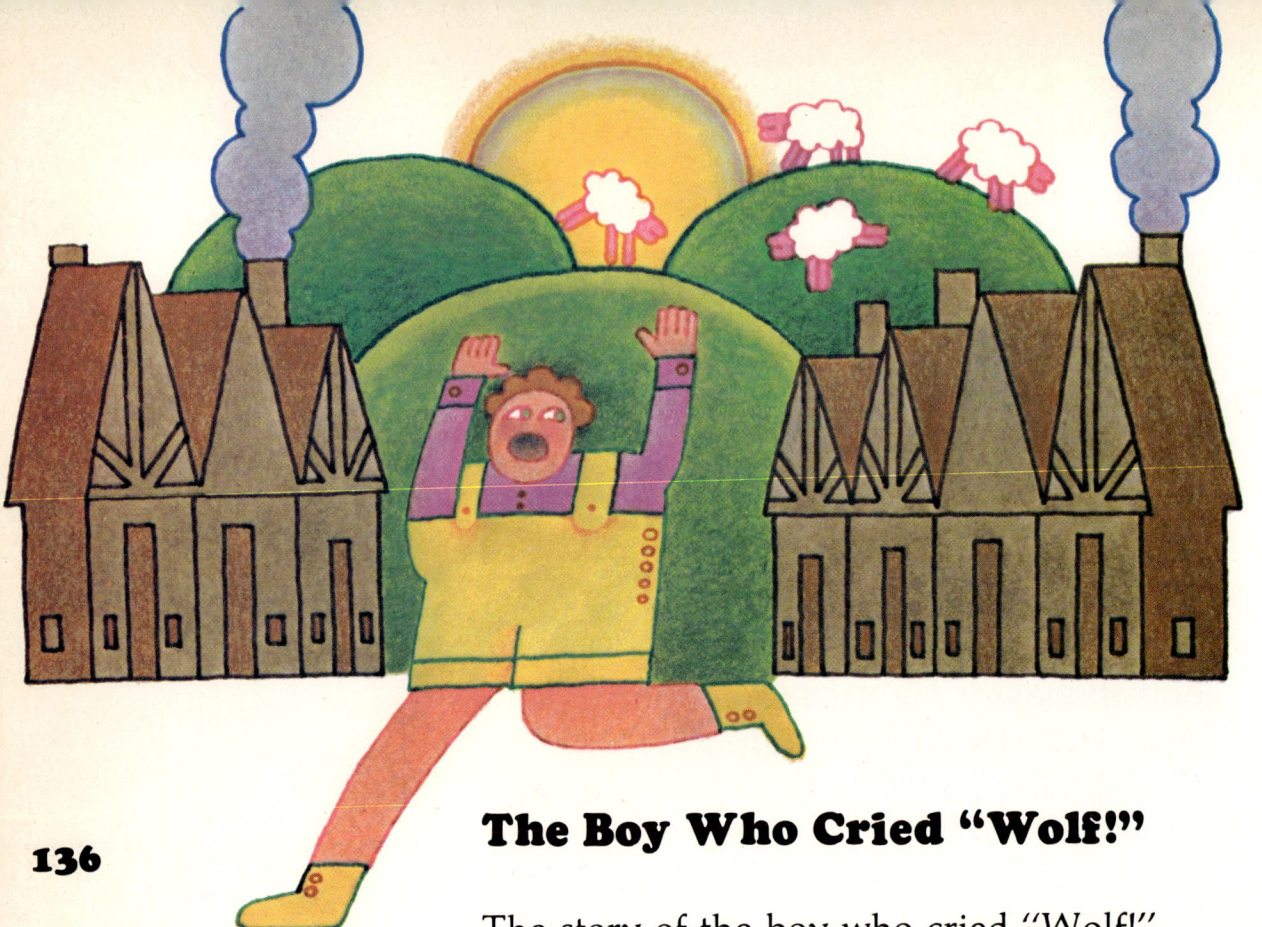

The Boy Who Cried "Wolf!"

The story of the boy who cried "Wolf!" reminds us of what happens to people who lie. This story also helps us to see what happens when we do not use our tongues correctly.

Once there was a boy who watched over a flock of sheep. He became lonely and bored. He wanted to stir up some excitement. So, he ran towards his village shouting, "Wolf! Wolf!"

The people from the village heard his cry. Waving their clubs and pitchforks, they ran to help. They followed the boy to the place where the wolf was supposed to be.

They saw no wolf. Still, they believed the boy when he said that the wolf must have run away.

Later the boy became bored again. So he ran towards the village a second time. He cried, "Wolf! Wolf!" Once again, the people ran to help. They followed the boy to the place where the wolf was supposed to be. This time, too, they found no wolf.

Later on, the boy was sitting alone among the sheep. He heard a sound. He looked up and really saw a wolf.

The boy sprang to his feet. He raced to the village as fast as he could go. He cried, "Wolf! Wolf!" at the top of his lungs. But people only looked at the boy. They smiled and went about their business. He had lied to them before. No one believed him now. So the wolf made a hearty meal of the sheep.

The boy complained. But the people told him, "Nobody believes a liar, even when he tells the truth."

St. James Teaches Us a Lesson

The Bible also tells us how to use our tongues. The Letter of St. James says:

> When we put bits into the mouths of horses to make them obey us, we guide the rest of their bodies.
>
> It is the same with ships. No matter how big they are, even if fierce winds are driving them, they are directed by very small rudders on whatever course the steersman's impulse may take.
>
> The tongue is something like that. It is small, yet it can proudly claim that it does great things.
>
> See how tiny the spark is that sets fire to a huge forest; the tongue is such a flame.
>
> We use it to say: "Blessed be the Lord and Father," then we use it to curse men who are made in the likeness of God. The blessing and the curse come out of the same mouth.
>
> My brothers, this must not be!

Stop and Think

We all know that we can hurt people with our words:

1. If you ever told a lie, can you remember what happened?

2. Why should you always speak the truth?

3. Has anyone ever hurt you with words? What did it feel like?

Ask Jesus to help you never to be mean with words.

For Home and School

1. In class talk about the following sayings:
   a. "A long tongue shortens life."
   b. "Though the tongue is boneless, it can break bones."

2. Can you name times when people's tongues have helped people or have hurt them?

3. Ask your parents to tell you about great speeches they have heard in the past. Did what they heard help them? How?

21. "You Shall Not Bear False Witness"

The Tower of Babel

The Hebrew children who lived thousands of years ago loved to hear stories. Best of all, they liked the stories their parents told them. These were stories about God, about the world, and about the people who lived long before. Some of these stories were written down. We can find them today in the Bible.

One of these stories was about the Tower of Babel. It told about what life was like after a great flood like the flood in the story of Noah. Once again, there were a great many people on earth. They all lived in the same area, and they all spoke the same language. They built up new villages and cities.

These people became very proud. They wanted to show everyone how great they were. They wanted even God to know of their greatness. They decided to build a tower that would reach far into the sky.

But God decided to teach these people a lesson. He mixed up their language. One person could no longer understand what another person was saying. One man might say, "Hand me a brick." The other would not understand. He might think his friend said it was time for lunch. The people could not help each other. They did not trust each other. They moved apart.

This story taught the Hebrew children many things. It teaches us many things, too. It teaches that people cannot work or live together if they cannot talk to one another. People cannot work or live together if they cannot understand one another. People must trust one another. They must tell the truth.

Words Count

God gave us tongues so that we can tell each other what we think. If we do not tell the truth, we lie. Lying divides people. When we lie to someone, we are not loving that person. We are cheating him. We are not being honest with him. We are saying one thing when we really mean something else. Jesus told us to be open and honest. He told us to say yes when we mean yes, and no when we mean no.

God wants people to live together in peace. When we call one another names, we misuse our tongues. God wants us to say nice things to others. He wants us to love each other. Then we can live together in peace.

There are many words which bring people closer together. People are pleased when they hear "Thank you." They like to hear "Excuse me." We all like to be told we have done something well. We like to have good things said about us. Kind words help us strive to become better people.

Stop and Think

The people who built the tower could no longer trust each other:

1. What does it mean to trust someone?

2. How do you act when you really trust?

3. Why should you trust people?

Ask Jesus to help you always tell the truth and to trust each other.

For Home and School

1. Do you remember a time when it took courage for you to tell the truth? Write a few sentences about it.

2. Saying one thing when you really mean something else only brings about distrust. Make up a play about the people who built the Tower. What were the people like before and after God mixed up their language?

3. On the back of a dollar bill, there is the motto, "IN GOD WE TRUST." What does it mean?

22. Share with One Another

We Learn to Share

Our parents teach us to share with one another. They do not want us to be greedy or selfish. They help us learn to do those things that Jesus told his friends to do.

Jesus said that when we give food, drink, or clothes to someone, we give them to Him:

> For I was hungry and you gave me food. I was thirsty and you gave me drink, naked and you clothed me.

There are many stories which tell about greedy people who will not share. Here are some of them.

The Greedy Dog

Once, a dog found a juicy piece of meat. He picked it up between his teeth. Then he started home to eat his meal in peace.

On the way, the dog had to cross a creek. As he walked on the log which stretched across, he looked down into the creek. The dog saw himself in the water. But he thought he was seeing another dog with another piece of meat. The dog said to himself, "I'll grab that piece from the other dog. Then I'll have two pieces."

The dog bent closer to the water. Then he opened his mouth to snap up the other piece of meat. But as soon as he opened his jaws, his piece of meat dropped into the water. It was lost forever.

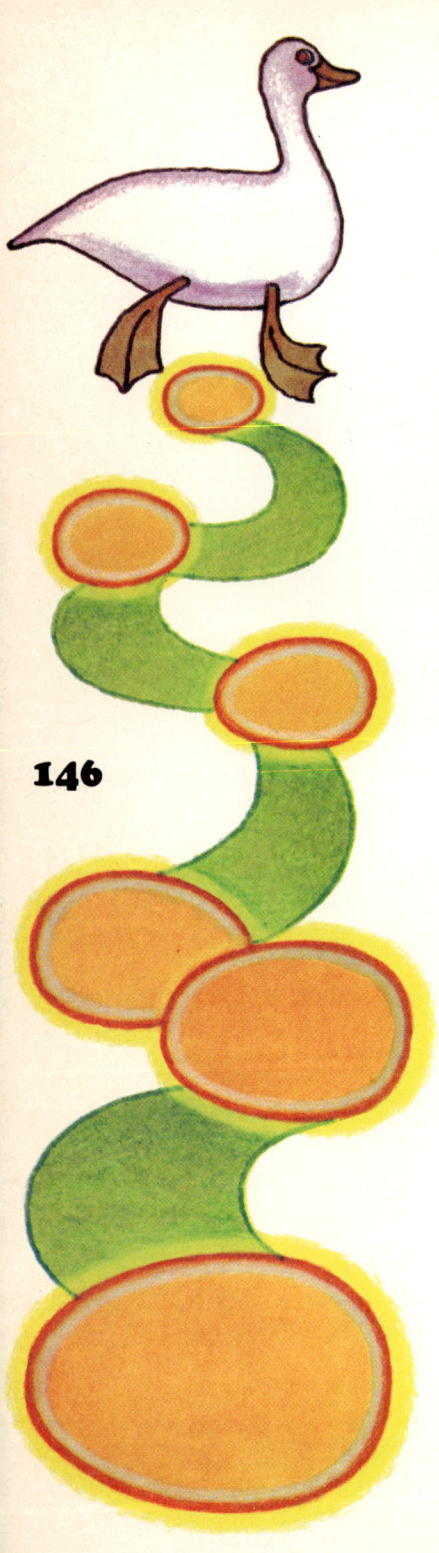

The Golden Eggs

A farmer bought a new goose. He put her in his barn. The next morning, he went to see the goose. He found that she had laid an egg. It was the size and shape of most any egg. But it was made of solid gold!

The farmer was wild with joy. He grabbed the egg and sold it for a lot of money. He bought many things his family needed.

The next morning, the farmer went to see the goose again. To his delight, she had laid another golden egg. Each morning, without fail, the farmer found a golden egg.

After a while, the farmer was a rich man. But, the richer he became, the richer he wanted to be. He grew tired of waiting for morning to get his golden egg.

"I think I'll have them all at once," the farmer said to himself one day. So he ran to the barn. He grabbed the goose and killed her. Then he opened up her stomach. But the greedy farmer found no golden eggs. There were only the insides of a dead goose.

Stop and Think

The greedy dog and the farmer teach us how important it is to share:

1. Have you ever wanted something very badly? When you got what you wanted, did you forget to share it with others?

2. Why do you think people should share what they have?

3. What can you do to become a person who shares?

Ask Jesus to help you always be a person who shares.

For Home and School

1. Should the greedy dog in the story have learned the saying, "A bird in the hand is worth two in the bush!"? What does this saying tell us?

2. Ask your parents to tell you a story about one person sharing what he has with another.

3. Ask your parents to read you the story Jesus told about the Good Samaritan (Luke 10:30—37). Discuss with your parents why it is a story about sharing and kindness.

23. "Lord, Teach Us How to Pray"

Words Bring Us Close to People

Helen Keller was a very pitiful girl. She became deaf and blind when she was a little baby. But not only was she unable to hear or see. She could not speak, either. She could not say "Please," or "Thank you." She could not say "I love you." She could not tell her mother or father how she felt. Helen could not say any of these things because she did not know a single word. She could not speak a word.

The world was a dark and silent place for little Helen. She was very lonely. Then, one day, Helen's parents heard about a special teacher. Her name was Annie Sullivan. Helen's parents asked her to help their little girl.

Annie Sullivan worked with Helen for a long time. She helped Helen touch things like tables and chairs and cups and spoons. Helen touched these things with one hand. She put two fingers of her other hand on her teacher's lips. Then Annie formed the

words for these things with her lips. With her fingers, Helen could feel how Annie's lips were moving. Helen tried to move her own lips the same way.

After a long time and much hard work, Helen was able to learn a few words. With each new word, she became more eager, more excited. Finally, she found that she could talk. She could tell her mother and father how she felt.

Now Helen was not so lonely. She could talk to the people she loved. She could reach out to them. She could tell them what she needed. She could say, "I love you."

Words Help Us to Pray

People like to talk to those they love. This is the reason people pray. When they pray, people talk to God. They reach out to God. They tell Him that they love Him. They ask Him for things they need. They thank Him.

Jesus would often go off by Himself and talk to His Father. Sometimes He spent the whole night praying.

One day, the apostles saw Jesus praying. He looked so peaceful when He prayed. There was such hope and love in His eyes.

The apostles wished that they could talk to God as Jesus did. They went to Him and said, "Lord, teach us how to pray."

Jesus told the apostles that when they wanted to pray, they should try to be by themselves. They should have a quiet time with God. He said that fancy words were not important. Instead, Jesus told them to talk to God as a child talks to his loving father.

The apostles took Jesus's advice. They learned to talk to God. They felt closer to God when they talked to Him in prayer.

Stop and Think

The story of Helen Keller tells us how important words can be. We can also use words to talk to God:

1. What do you talk to your parents about?

2. Have you ever felt like talking to God?

3. How do you talk to God?

4. Why should we talk to God?

Take a minute right now to talk to God in your own words.

For Home and School

1. Make up some prayers that you can say:
    a. before meals.
    b. after meals.
    c. before you go to sleep.
    d. when you wake up.

2. St. Clement said, "Prayer is conversation with God." Discuss what St. Clement meant.

3. Ask your parents to read to you what Jesus said about praying (*Matthew 6:5—15*).

24. Let Us Pray

We Celebrate Together

Celebration!
What comes to your mind when you think of that word?
Do you think of a birthday party, with everyone wearing paper hats and eating cake and ice cream together?
Do you think of a family picnic on the Fourth of July, with everyone enjoying a meal out in the open and watching fireworks together?
There are other pictures that could come to mind, too. But no matter what celebration we think of, one thing is always true. It must be people doing something *together*. People don't celebrate alone. They celebrate with other people.
Jesus told His friends to pray to God by themselves. But He also told His friends to pray *together*. He promised that when they prayed together, He would be there with them.

When We Pray, We Celebrate

When we go to church, we come together to celebrate. We gather in the church to pray as a family, God's Family. We talk to God as one. We listen to God's word. We sing as a family. God wants His children to come together. That is why He asks them to meet and pray *together.*

People celebrate and pray together at different times and in different ways. Families gather to celebrate Baptism in church.

People come for penance services. They say they are sorry for their sins and ask God to forgive them. They come especially for the Eucharistic Celebration on Sundays and holy days.

When people gather together, they help one another. It helps people to pray when others pray with them. Praying together makes people feel that they are all members of God's Family.

Stop and Think

The Mass is a very special prayer. It is a celebration of many things we share as a believing Family:

1. How do you feel when you go to Mass?

2. Why do you think people should go to Mass?

3. What can you do at Mass?

Thank Jesus for the Mass, the special way we have of remembering Him and receiving Him as the Bread of Life.

For Home and School

1. Make up your own poem which tells how you feel about the Eucharistic Celebration.

2. Ask your parents to tell you about people who love the Eucharist.

3. Can you name times in which we, as Catholics, come together to pray besides at baptisms and at the Eucharistic Celebration?

4. Ask your parents to tell you ways in which you can prepare for receiving the Bread of Life during the Eucharistic Celebration.

25. "I Am Sorry"

The Wooden and the Real Pinocchios

Pinocchio was all alone. After all his adventures and troubles, the little wooden puppet had come home at last. But the house was dark, cold, and empty.

Why was this cheerful, lively place so sad and empty? A note on the table told Pinocchio why. He picked up the note and read:

> I have gone to look for my little wooden Pinocchio. I do not know when I will be back.
> Gepetto, the Toymaker

As he read the note, Pinocchio felt his eyes burning. His wooden eyes were trying to do something they had never done before. They wanted to do something they could not do. They were trying to cry.

Now Pinocchio felt something he had not known before. He felt sorrow. "I caused all this," Pinocchio said to himself. "I have made my good father unhappy. I have lost him. I don't know where he is."

Later, Pinocchio learned that his father had been swallowed by a huge whale. Pinocchio felt even worse. Then he said something he had never said before. "I am sorry," Pinocchio said. "I must find my poor father. I must tell him how sorry I am."

Pinocchio did find his father. He rescued the toymaker from the whale's belly. He told his father that he was sorry.

Pinocchio felt sad that he had caused the Fairy with the Blue Hair trouble, too. Once again, he said, "I am sorry." He gave the fairy some money he had saved.

The day Pinocchio was able to feel sorry because he had hurt someone was the day Pinocchio became a real boy.

Becoming a Better Boy or Girl

The story of Pinocchio is just a story. Everyone knows that wooden puppets do not become real boys. But the story tells us something which is very important. It reminds us that we become better persons when we learn to be unselfish, thoughtful, and obedient.

Every real boy and girl has a conscience. The conscience tells them what is good and bad. It tells them how to do what is pleasing to God. It tells them how to please their parents and other people who love them.

Real boys and girls know something Pinocchio did not know. They know that God loves them. They know that God wants them to become better every day. They know that they are God's children and He is their Father.

It is sometimes hard to be unselfish. It is hard to think of others instead of one's self. It is hard to obey. But real boys and girls get a reward greater than Pinocchio's. They are happy because they know that God is pleased with them.

Stop and Think

Sometimes it is very hard to tell someone that we are sorry:

1. Why should you say you are sorry when you hurt someone?

2. How can you show your parents that you are sorry for not obeying them?

3. How do you show God that you are sorry for not having listened to Him?

Ask Jesus to help you tell how sorry you are.

For Home and School

1. Discuss in class the saying, "Let your conscience be your guide."

2. Make a list of things that you will try to do for your family and friends during the summer. Share the list with your parents.

Special People, Special Times

Everybody knows some special people. Family members, characters in a book, and heroes of TV shows are all special to us. We have special memories of these people. We share special times with them.

The Church is like that too. In its long history, there have been many special people. They have memories and customs, games and songs connected with them.

Some of the Church's special times, like Christmas and Easter, are familiar to us. We know some of the special people, like Mary, already. In this section, we meet some of the other special people. We share some of the other special times.

A Birthday for Mary

The Special Day

It was the eighth day of September. Autumn was about to begin. Anton was excited, because this year he was old enough to be a real "senne," or shepherd.

In the Alps in Switzerland where Anton lived, it was too cold to let the cows stay outside all winter. They spent the snowy months in warm barns, feeding on hay and corn.

Bringing the cows down from the mountain meadows was fun. It was a big celebration. And every year, it happened on the same day as the Blessed Mother's birthday.

Of course, no one really knew what day Mary had been born on. But ever since anyone could remember, September 8th meant two things in Anton's village: Mary's birthday and the day the cows came down.

All the way down the mountain, the

shepherds sang old songs. Anton yodeled and then listened to his voice bouncing off the sides of the mountains. He loved to make echoes.

It was evening when they reached the town. The animals were given lots of good feed. Anton joined his family at their party table in the town square. He ate roast chicken and cake, and he had a little taste of wine.

Then he helped gather up all the leftover food. With the milk from the cows, it would be given to the poor and the sick in honor of Mary's birthday.

Before bed, everyone went to church. The priest blessed the corn and grain from the harvest, and the first grapes. People tied some of the grapes to the hands of the statue of the Blessed Mother. That way they remembered all the things they were celebrating.

Just before Anton fell asleep, he felt a little sad. Mary's birthday was the end of summer. But then he smiled to himself. Next spring, he would be the first one to lead the animals back up the mountain.

People of Light: Christmas

The Kind Old Bishop

The old Bishop Nicholas was walking one night in his town in what is now the country of Turkey. Suddenly, he heard weeping coming through the open window of a house. He couldn't help overhearing what was going on inside.

What Nicholas heard made him sad. The poor man who lived in the house was telling his three daughters that he could not afford to give them big weddings. The girls were crying. In their town, girls needed lots of money to get married. Nobody would marry poor girls.

Nicholas knew what to do. He went home and filled three sacks with gold coins. Then he went back to the poor man's house. He didn't let anyone see him. One by one, Nicholas tossed the sacks of gold coins through the open window.

The poor man thought it was a miracle. Now his daughters could get married. But one of them had seen Nicholas. She thanked him, and word spread all over of how generous the bishop was.

The Sailor's Friend

Another time, long after Nicholas' death, some sailors were lost in a storm. One of them remembered the kind old bishop and asked for his help. The storm stopped. It soon became a custom for sailors all over the world to steer by the "star of Saint Nicholas."

Some of the greatest sailors in the world were people from Holland. They brought home the story of the kind old bishop. The feast of Saint Nicholas, December 6th, is celebrated all over Europe, but especially in Holland. Children put their shoes on the windowsill and believe that Nicholas fills them with candy and little presents.

On that day in Holland, an old man dresses like a bishop and sails into the harbor cities. He blesses the boats. Then he rides through town on a white horse, tossing chocolate "gold pieces" to the crowds.

Santa Claus

The sailors of Holland came to America. And they brought Saint Nicholas' story here. To the English, "Saint Nicholas" in Dutch sounded more like "Santa Claus." Long ago, a newspaper cartoonist drew a picture of Nicholas. He made him look more like a plump old sailor instead of a bishop. We still picture Santa Claus as a fat man riding in a sleigh, instead of on a white horse.

Turnips and Stars

In other Northern countries in Europe, the light of Christmas also has a special meaning. In Northern Canada, families store turnips in the snow after the fall harvest. At Christmas, each child is given a turnip with a candle stuck into it. The candles are made of flavored honeycombs, so the children eat up the whole thing!

The Eskimos of Alaska have a special caroling custom. They carry a big paper lantern in the shape of a star. At each house, they sing carols and are given treats. But between houses, they have to run from other children. These children are dressed like the soldiers of King Herod, and they race to try and "capture" the star of Bethlehem!

Groundhogs, Candles and Wolves

The Groundhog

On February 2nd, children and farmers wait to see the groundhog come out of his hole. An old story says that if the sun is shining, the little animal gets scared by his shadow. He jumps back into his hole, and everybody groans. Then people know that spring will be a long time coming.

But if the day is cloudy, the groundhog stays out to play. And everyone laughs, because spring is coming soon.

Of course, groundhogs don't really know anything about the weather. But for hundreds and hundreds of years, people have watched the skies on February 2nd.

"A Light to the World"

Maybe Mary looked up at the skies on that day, a long time ago. It was the first time she had been out of the house since Jesus' birth. Then, women weren't allowed out in public for forty days after having a baby. On the fortieth day, a new mother brought an animal, like a lamb, to sacrifice at the Temple.

Joseph and Mary couldn't afford a lamb, so they brought two pigeons. And they brought Jesus.

One of the people who saw Him at the Temple had some strange things to say. "This child is from God!" said Simeon, an old man. "He will be a light to the whole world!"

For hundreds of years, Christians have kept that light alive. February 2nd is called "Candlemas," or Candle Day. It has always been a day to march around the church, carrying candles. The candles were blessed by the priest and then carried home. Throughout the year, they were lit to give hope, when people were sick or when there was a storm.

Mary's Thunder Candle

In Poland, February 2nd is a day of deep snow and cold winds. Long ago, people sat in their dark homes and heard the wolves outside in the forest. But they were not afraid. They believed that the Blessed Mother walked through the woods. She carried a candle that burned with the sound of thunder. It frightened all the wolves away. Some Polish people call Mary, "The Lady of the Thunder Candle."

Fishbones and Blessings

The Friend of Wild Animals

Hundreds and hundreds of years ago, a bishop named Blaise went to live in the forest. He fled from people who did not believe in Jesus and who wanted to kill him. So Blaise found a cave in the forest and moved in.

Blaise spent a long time in the forest. After a while, he knew a lot about the wild

animals. He named each one and fed all of them. The animals trusted Blaise because he was quiet and he lived simply like they did. Whenever an animal was sick or wounded, it came to Blaise. And Blaise took care of it.

Word spread about the man who could heal animals. But Blaise's enemies found out where he was. They sent soldiers to bring Blaise to jail.

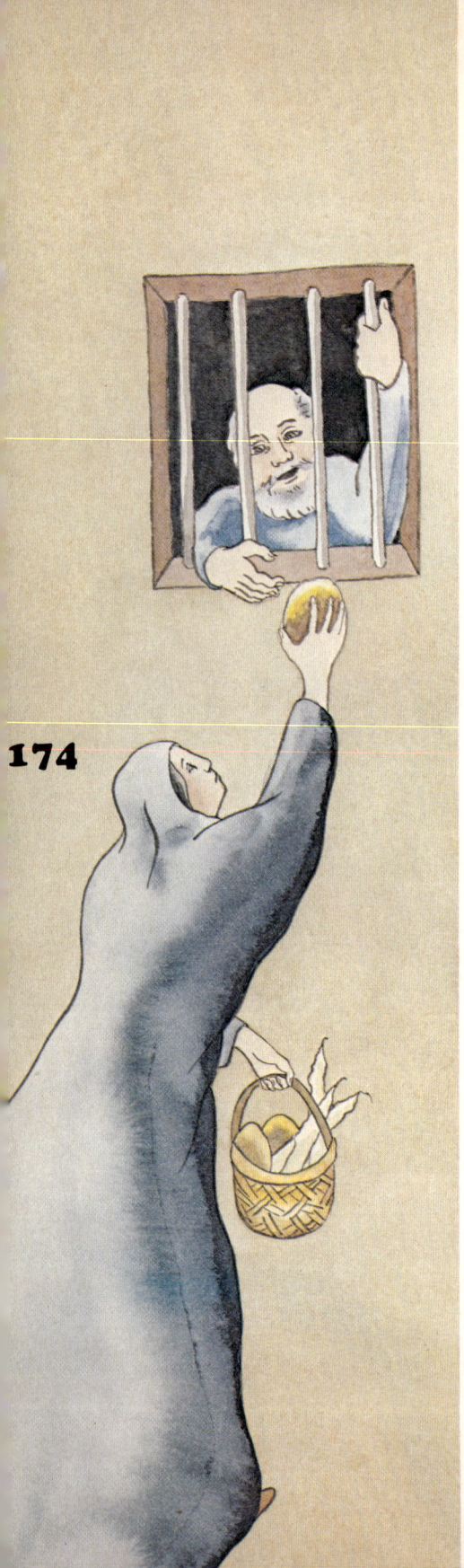

On the way out of the forest, Blaise and the soldiers saw a woman. She was crying and was very worried. She told them she was very poor. A wild wolf had just run off with her pig, the only farm animal she had.

Blaise called out. The wild wolf came out of the forest. It was walking like a lamb, and it brought back the woman's pig unharmed.

The woman was very happy. She always remembered Blaise. All the time he was in jail, she visited him. And even though she was poor, she brought him food and candles.

The Fishbone

While Blaise was in jail, a rich man's son became very sick. He seemed to stop breathing. The man had heard how well Blaise could cure people and animals. So he brought his son to the jail.

Blaise touched the boy's throat, and out jumped a fishbone that had been stuck there. The boy was cured!

Later, Blaise was put to death by his enemies. But, he became famous for curing people. And he was made a saint. Most people remember Saint Blaise because of the fishbone. In Italy, people make little bone-shaped cakes called "pan bendito," blessed bread, to eat on his feast day, February 3.

A very old custom of the Church is the blessing of throats. On Saint Blaise's feast day, people come to the church. The priest crosses two unlit candles and holds them next to each person's throat. (They are like the candles Blaise's friend brought to him in jail.) Then the priest says a prayer:

> *"Through the help of Saint Blaise, bishop and martyr, may God deliver you from ailments of the throat, and from every other evil.*

In Saint Blaise's day, people didn't know much about medicine or how to stay healthy. Often, they prayed to holy people to help them to stay well. The story of Saint Blaise can be a reminder to us to take care of our health.

Patrick in the Halls of Tara: Easter

*I bind to myself today
God's power to guide me,
God's might to unhold me,
God's eye to watch over me.*

Patrick sat on a rock and frowned. God had sent him to Ireland. But most of the Irish didn't want to listen to him. It was the day before Easter, the holiest time of all. And Patrick had to find a way to make people hear his message.

It was very dark. The king of Ireland, who lived in his castle at Tara, had made a law. The law said that no fires could be lit for the whole week before Easter. The king wanted to be sure that his magicians would be the only ones able to light the new fire, the sign of a new spring in their religion. Sitting around in the dark at night made the people very frightened of evil spirits and ghosts and dead people.

Patrick wanted to tell the people that